T0319566

Communication Essentials for Financial Planners

Communication Essentials for Financial Planners

Strategies and Techniques

JOHN E. GRABLE
JOSEPH W. GOETZ

WILEY

Edited by

Charles R. Chaffin, EdD

Library of Congress Cataloging-in-Publication Data

Names: Grable, John E., author. | Goetz, Joseph W. (Professor of financial planning), author.
Title: Communication essentials for financial planners : strategies and techniques / John E. Grable, Joseph W. Goetz.
Description: Hoboken, New Jersey : John Wiley & Sons, Inc., [2017] | Includes bibliographical references and index. |
Identifiers: LCCN 2017001119 (print) | LCCN 2017016280 (ebook) | ISBN 9781119350798 (pdf) | ISBN 9781119350774 (epub) | ISBN 9781119350781 (cloth)
Subjects: LCSH: Financial planners. | Interpersonal communication. | Interpersonal relations. | Investment advisor-client relationships.
Classification: LCC HG179.5 (ebook) | LCC HG179.5 .G695 2017 (print) | DDC 332.6—dc23
LC record available at https://lccn.loc.gov/2017001119

Contents

Preface

For financial planners . . . communication . . . is the single most powerful antecedent to trust and commitment . . .
—Dr. Dave Yeske[1]

The purpose of this book is to provide financial planners with insights on how they can improve their communication and counseling skills. The approach presented in this book is based on helping financial planners develop, practice, and use skills associated with the formal and informal sharing of information between a client and the financial planning professional in an empathic manner that enhances the client–financial planner relationship.[2]

This book serves as a valuable resource for students and professionals alike. The ineffable importance of consistent and effective communication with clients is widely acknowledged by experienced financial planners. At the same time, few planners have implemented systems within their firms (or personal professional development plans) to increase knowledge and hone skills associated with client communication! This book provides professional financial planners, as well as the leadership within financial planning firms, with a blueprint for taking their client communication to the next level. Inarguably, increased sophistication in client communication translates to higher client retention and a more effective financial planning process. Thus, the ROI on time allocated to toward communication skill development is quite high.

Those who conduct research on financial counseling and planning also know that communication skills are the foundation to building a successful financial planning practice. Some researchers have even contended that, "effective communication is vital to successful financial planning."[3] Certified Financial Planner Board of Standards Inc. (CFP Board)—the primary academic standards setting and enforcement board for college and university programs[4]—supports this notion, as it has identified *communication and counseling skills* as an essential element of *financial planning competency*.

WHY THIS BOOK

Over the past two decades, myriad financial planning practitioners have emphasized the importance of client communication to business success and client satisfaction.[5] In fact, the authors, who regularly hear practitioners speak about their professional roles when invited by their university's student financial planning organization, have noticed a consistent emphasis on client communication and relationship building as the foundation of each presenter's success. Many of these practitioners believe strongly that their method of client communication is effective, and undoubtedly it is at some level, but what they may fail to consider is whether another communication strategy or skillset could work even better. As will be highlighted throughout this book, the study of communication and counseling skills can assist even those financial planners who are already quite proficient communicators to become even more effective in their work with clients.

Current financial planning practice standards mandate that anyone hoping to become a Certified Financial Planner (CFP®) professional must obtain proficiency in the following interpersonal communication domains:

- Evaluating client and planner attitudes, values, biases, and behavioral characteristics and the impact these have on financial planning
- Principles of communication and counseling

The CFP Board's requirement goes beyond a theoretical understanding to requiring proficiency. The role of communicating effectively with prospective and current clients permeates the financial planning process. Consider the CFP Board's standards related to professional conduct and fiduciary responsibility, disciplinary rules and procedures, and practice standards. According to the CFP Board, practice standards are intended to:

1. Assure that the practice of financial planning by CFP® professionals is based on established norms of practice
2. Advance professionalism in financial planning
3. Enhance the value of the financial planning process

Practice standards apply to all CFP® professionals and those studying financial planning in a CFP Board Registered Program. The standards, however, also serve as a foundation for professionalism within the broader financial services profession. Practice standards were first developed in 1987, updated in 1994 by CTB/McGraw-Hill, an independent consulting firm, and again in 1999 by the Chauncey Group. These standards, tied directly to steps in the financial planning process, are shown in Table P.1.

TABLE P.1   The Financial Planning Process and Related Practice Standards

Financial Planning Process	Related Practice Standard
1. Establishing and defining the relationship with a client	100-1 Defining the Scope of the Engagement
2. Gathering client data	200-1 Determining a Client's Personal and Financial Goals, Needs, and Priorities
	200-2 Obtaining Quantitative Information and Documents
3. Analyzing and evaluating the client's financial status	300-1 Analyzing and Evaluating the Client's Information
4. Developing and presenting financial planning recommendations	400-1 Identifying and Evaluating Financial Planning Alternative(s)
	400-2 Developing the Financial Planning Recommendation(s)
	400-3 Presenting the Financial Planning Recommendation(s)
5. Implementing the financial planning recommendations	500-1 Agreeing on Implementation Responsibilities
	500-2 Selecting Products and Services for Implementation
6. Monitoring	600-1 Defining Monitoring Responsibilities

Source: CFP Board, 2016: www.cfp.net/for-cfp-professionals/professional-standards-enforcement/standards-of-professional-conduct.

What is important to remember, from the perspective of this book, is the role communication and counseling skills play at each step in the financial planning process. Imagine how challenging it might be for some financial planners if they needed to meet a prospective client who is unsure of his or her need for financial planning because of cultural or ethnic barriers. Without a systematic approach that can be used to build rapport through questions, feedback, and encouragement, this meeting could end up being a lost opportunity for both the client and the financial planner. Not only could the financial planner lose a potential client, the prospective client may shy away from needed behavioral change. The importance of applying appropriate communication and counseling techniques at each step of the financial planning process is just as important. As it turns out, not only are communication and counseling skills important attributes of professionalism, these skills often determine who has the greatest likelihood of becoming a client's most trusted adviser.

Five *communication tasks*—or functions every financial planner needs to perform—have been linked in the academic literature directly with the CFP Board's practice standards[6]:

1. Mutually defining the scope of an engagement before providing financial planning advice
2. Helping clients identify meaningful personal and financial goals
3. Applying a systematic communication and counseling process that helps clients clarify their financial and life goals
4. Taking time to explore and learn about each client's cultural background, personality, attitudes, beliefs, and family history and values
5. Explaining how financial advice aligns with each client's unique values, goals, and needs

Financial planners who embrace these five communication tasks with each client report greater client retention, higher client satisfaction, greater client cooperation, more openness in discussions, greater client disclosure, and more referrals.

While it is true that the CFP board requires all financial planning professionals who hold the CFP® marks, as well as those studying for CFP® certification, to exhibit communication and counseling proficiency, the purpose of studying communication and counseling is much more profound. Essentially, the manner in which a financial planner reaches out to others determines, to a large extent, that professional's effectiveness in helping clients make life-changing decisions. We are not talking about helping salespeople sell one additional product or service as the end result, but rather, facilitating the growing professionalism of financial planning in the marketplace. Just as attorneys, accountants, and physicians must employ communication and counseling skills on a daily basis, the same is true for professional financial planners. An important outcome associated with reading this book, watching the accompanying videos, and practicing each chapter's techniques should be a greater appreciation on the fundamental skill sets needed to be a competent financial planner in the twenty-first century.

COMMUNICATION: WHAT IS IT?

Before moving forward, it is worth pausing and clarifying exactly what this book is all about. The word *communication* is very broad and used in multiple ways in the financial planning profession. Communication can be broken down into four domains:

- Communication methods
- Communication tasks
- Communication topics
- Communication skills

Much of the financial planning literature relative to communication really focuses on *methods of communication,* such as using a phone, email, blogs, face-to-face meetings, newsletters, mailers, social media, and group functions. All of those elements are important to client engagement, but there is much more to becoming a truly proficient communicator. *Communication tasks* encompass a variety of procedures and practice standards (for example, explaining how advice matches a client's goals and objectives). It is important to note that *communication topics* can vary from client to client, including conversations about a client's values, for example, to discussions regarding specific products and procedures. While these three elements of communication are very important, this book is focused more intently on the *purpose of communication* and *communication and counseling skills* (e.g., verbal, nonverbal, and spatial skills). Table P.2 illustrates the difference between communication tasks and communication and counseling skills. As noted earlier, the focus of this book is squarely on the skills needed to be an effective financial planner.

Even though this book only tangentially touches on methods, tasks, and topics of communication, the research surrounding the usefulness of these communication elements is astounding and worth reviewing. When asked, nearly 50 percent of practicing financial planners have historically indicated that they spend between 9 and 14 hours per week communicating with

TABLE P.2 Communication Tasks and Skills Compared

Tasks	Skills
Defining the scope of the relationship	Asking thoughtful questions
Communicating planners' attributes	Observing client body language
Gathering demographic client data	Practicing listening skills
Gathering financial client data	Using strategic questions
Helping client identify meaningful goals	Arranging office to reduce client stress
Explaining planning recommendations	Maintaining eye contact with client

Source: Adapted from Sharpe et al. (2007).

clients.[7] Financial planners who claim the greatest success in growing their practice, however, report communicating directly with clients at least 30 to 34 hours per week. The most popular (not necessarily the best) methods of communication include the telephone, email, face-to-face meetings, and newsletters. The reasons for communicating are diverse, including reviewing a client's goals, evaluating portfolio performance, providing advice, discussing life events, staying in touch, providing market commentary, and educating clients. Some financial planners also use methods of communication to ask for referrals.

The number of hours successful financial planners spend communicating with clients sometimes surprises aspiring financial planners. It is a common belief that financial planners spend the majority of their time devoted to evaluating quantitative data. While this may be true for some financial planners—particularly those who work in larger firms where task specialties are the norm—the most successful financial planners tend to devote less than 50 percent of their working day to quantitative issues. More time is spent on coaching and counseling activities.[8] As an example, the following communication tasks and topics are frequently reported as being important when building long-lasting and committed client–financial planner relationships[9]:

- Counseling a client who is emotionally distraught
- Mediating between husband and wife
- Mediating between client and children
- Prompting a client to seek therapy
- Encouraging a client's family member to seek therapy
- Discussing prayer and God with some clients
- Acting as a keeper of client secrets
- Lobbying a client to engage in philanthropic activities

It should be obvious that communication skills are at the root of all impactful financial planning services. Based on the existing literature, it is hardly a stretch to conclude that communication and counseling skills are among the most important characteristics separating successful financial planners from others.

BUILDING CLIENT TRUST AND COMMITMENT

Appropriate use of communication methods can also go a long way to building *client trust and commitment*.[10] Although there are many factors that help cement a client–financial planner relationship, five stand out as being very important:

1. Taking time to understand a client's needs and concerns
2. Fully understanding a client's goals
3. Providing each client with peace of mind
4. Clearly explaining difficult concepts
5. Placing the client's needs above all else when making recommendations[11]

In regard to methods of communication, being predictable is of critical importance.[12]

A financial planner must be able to communicate effectively to bring these five factors together. For those financial planners who want to build client trust and commitment, developing and practicing outstanding client communication and counseling skills is the most effective path to this outcome.[13]

MODELS OF COMMUNICATION

Researchers working over the past half century have built numerous models that help explain the process of communication. Almost every model extends the basic *rhetorical framework* originally proposed by Aristotle, as shown in Figure P.1.

The components of the model are self-explanatory. The sender is the person who originates the interchange. The message consists of the content being delivered. The receiver is the person to whom the message is sent.

It should be clear that several important features are missing from Figure P.1. Of particular importance is the *channel of exchange*. In Aristotle's time, the channel or medium of exchange tended to be either oral or written. Today, of course, there are many different channels through which two or more people can communicate. It is helpful to think of a channel matching up to one of the five senses: hearing, seeing, feeling, tasting, or smelling. Taken more broadly, the channel of communication provides a mechanism to deliver a message.

Messages are composed of *information, elements* (that is, words, sounds, gestures, images, and so forth); *structures* (that is, the composition of different elements); and *codes* (that is, the "language" of delivery words, tones, smells, music, and so forth).

FIGURE P.1   Aristotle's Original Communication Model

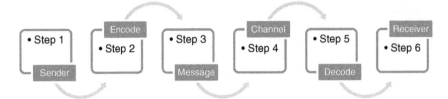

FIGURE P.2   Berlo's SMCR Communication Model

Essentially, a sender encodes his or her message, chooses a channel to transmit the message, and sends the message. The receiver decodes the message. The decoding process will always be influenced by the receiver's fluency in the language used by the sender and the receiver's attitude when the message is received. Embedded in the *encoding* and *decoding* process are issues related to shared values, beliefs, language, culture, cognitive ability, experience, and knowledge. Berlo[14] incorporated the concepts of sender, receiver, message, channel, encoding, and decoding to propose what he termed the SMCR communication model, which is shown in Figure P.2.

Many adaptations to the SMCR framework have been proposed over the years. Advances include the inclusion of feedback loops from the receiver to the sender and more nuanced descriptions of encoding and decoding. This book adds to this discussion by proposing a financial planning communication and counseling skills framework. The framework was built using many of the concepts found in the SMCR model. The framework is described in more detail next.

FINANCIAL PLANNING COMMUNICATION AND COUNSELING SKILLS FRAMEWORK

The purpose of presenting a communication and counseling skills framework is to provide readers with a tool to help conceptualize the way in which a financial planner interacts with prospective and current clients. This book is primarily focused on helping financial planners encode, send, receive, and decode messages. While some attention is given to the channel of communication, the real emphasis of the book is devoted to exploring the inner workings of the framework shown in Figure P.3.

The following example provides a step-by-step review of the financial planning communication and counseling process.

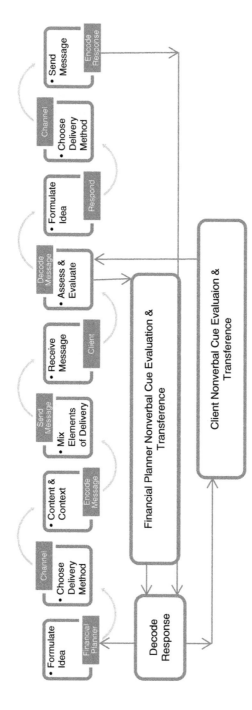

FIGURE P.3 Financial Planning Communication and Counseling Framework

Step 1

At Step 1, a financial planner formulates an idea to communicate with or to a client. For illustrative purposes, assume a financial planner intends to assess a client's risk tolerance. Issues related to explaining what risk tolerance means, the reason for the assessment, and the best technique to evaluate the client's risk tolerance need to be addressed. It is possible that some of this work will have been completed before the point of initial client communication.

Step 2

At Step 2, the financial planner needs to choose a channel for delivering her message about risk tolerance to the client. Assuming the client and financial planner are meeting together, the delivery channel may be a combination of verbal—using a question—and tactile—having the client complete a brief questionnaire. It is important to note that this step in the process differs from other communication models. Typically, message development is the second step in the communication process. In practice, Steps 2 and 3 (channel and message) are somewhat fluid. Consider a situation in which a financial planner wants to provide an immediate market update to her clients. Choosing the channel first is appropriate as a way to edit the content of the message. For example, using a group email will require different message content than a decision to call each client separately. There is flexibility built into the framework, however, for situations that require content to precede channel selection.

Step 3

At Step 3, the financial planner then needs to formalize the content and context of the message. Using the risk tolerance example, the content will include information about risk tolerance and the need to accurately assess the client's risk attitude in the context of the financial planning engagement. Issues related to language, cultural sensitivity, and client skills also need to be incorporated into the message. Given the choice of channel, appropriate context needs to be considered. Consider how the word *risk* can be interpreted differently by people based on their values, preferences, beliefs, and cultural background. For some, risk can be perceived as an opportunity. For others, risk is considered to be just a softer word to describe a loss. The financial planner may decide to ask the following question: "Tell me, how would your best friend describe you as a risk taker?" After the client responds, the financial planner could then present the risk questionnaire.

Step 4

Sending the message—Step 4—is of particular importance. The financial planner needs to mix the elements of delivery to most effectively communicate what is being asked and needed. Elements include words, tones, gestures, expressions, images, and body language. In this example, the financial planner may simply use her voice and encouraging facial expressions to reassure the client when answering a question. This can be followed by physically handing the risk questionnaire to the client and then leaning away from the client to provide space for a response.

Steps 5 and 6

Once the message has been sent, it is up to the client to receive and decode the message—Steps 5 and 6. These steps in the process happen quickly and are usually based on the type of question asked and the client's personal beliefs, values, cultural background, preferences, and expectations, in addition to other factors. While it is easy to think about these steps theoretically, it is important to remain grounded in practice. Everyone uses eye contact, body position, and other forms of nonverbal communication during a conversation. Being able to identify and use these forms of communication is an essential element in the process of building client trust and commitment.

While the client is receiving and decoding the message, there will be opportunities for the planner to observe *nonverbal cues*. These are essentially unspoken signals sent back to the financial planner. It is important to note that very rarely are the cues purposeful or intentional. These cues, however, can serve as important clues about the message's success or failure. Consider, for example, sending an email to a client. If a client responds immediately, this might indicate that the client is interested in the message. It might, on the other hand, simply mean that the client was online when the message was delivered. A delayed response could indicate a lukewarm interest in the message. It could also indicate that the client does not read his or her email often, and as such, a different channel of delivery is needed. Identifying and interpreting these nonverbal cues is an important financial planning communication skill.

In addition to nonverbal cues, financial planners need to be aware of a phenomenon called *transference*. Sometimes a client's attitude, mood, fear, or other emotional disposition is communicated nonverbally back to the financial planner during the client's decoding process. If unaddressed, the client's disposition can be absorbed or taken on by the financial planner. It is important for financial planners to understand when this occurs and how to handle this possibility. The arrow running from nonverbal cue evaluation and transference to the box called "decode response" represents the ongoing continuous feedback dynamic that is active in nearly every client–financial planner communication and counseling situation.

Steps 7 and 8

Whenever dialog occurs, the client (or receiver of a message) automatically engages in an assessment and evaluation of the message. As shown in Figure 3, at Step 7 the client formulates his or her own idea in response to the message. Within a financial planning engagement, this step in the process will hopefully be engaging and productive. There may be times, however, when no response is given. The client then moves to Step 8. This involves selecting a channel for response. The client then sends his or her response message back to the financial planner at Step 9.

Step 9

Although Step 9 represents the last stage in the process, the actual communication and counseling framework is continuous, as shown with the arrow from Step 9 back to the financial planner decode response box. Stated another way, the framework is built on multiple levels of feedback. This is illustrated with the arrow coming from the financial planner's decode response box back to the client at Step 6. This represents the client's own interpretation and evaluation of nonverbal cues being sent by the financial planner. For example, imagine what the client would think if, during the evaluation of risk tolerance discussion, the financial planner started talking to someone else on her cell phone? It is likely that the client's trust and commitment would be harmed.

SUMMARY

As illustrated in Figure P.3, the financial planning communication and counseling process is potentially endless. Of course, there may be times when a particular communication has a demonstrated beginning and ending point. Asking a client, for example, if he or she would like some coffee or tea, may not lead to an ongoing discussion with feedback experiences. The fact that the question was asked and answered, however, adds to the ongoing client–financial planner engagement.

The remainder of this book reviews some of the most important communication and counseling skills that researchers and successful financial planners have identified as being essential to becoming an effective and successful financial planner in the twenty-first century. Throughout the book, we provide examples of important techniques as well as contexts in which some of these actions transpire in practice. In many situations, video examples of what to do and what to avoid are also provided. It is through a combination of reading, watching, and practicing that a financial planner can improve his or her skillset. Whether in your final day of your thirtieth year in financial planning or your first day in your first year of enrollment in a CFP Board Registered Program, we strongly believe this book will facilitate useful reflection regarding best avenues for engaging clients or for you beginners, allow you to build an important skillset that is the keystone element of serving our clients.

NOTES

1. D. Yeske, "Finding the Planning in Financial Planning," *Journal of Financial Planning* 23, no. 10 (2010): 40–51.
2. N. Sharma and P. G. Patterson, "The Impact of Communication Effectiveness and Service Quality on Relationship Commitment in Consumer, Professional Services," *Journal of Services Marketing* 13 (1999): 151–171.
3. D. L. Sharpe, C. Anderson, A. White, S. Galvan, and M. Siesta, "Specific Elements of Communication That Affect Trust and Commitment in the Financial Planning Process," *Journal of Financial Counseling and Planning* 18, no. 1 (2007): 2–17.
4. "CFP Board is a professional certification and standards setting organization founded in 1985 to benefit the public by establishing and enforcing education, examination, experience, and ethics requirements for CFP professionals. Through its certification process, CFP Board established fundamental criteria necessary for competency in the financial planning profession."
5. H. Evensky, *Put Your Mouth Where Your Money Is: The 9 Keys to Proactive and Interactive Communication for a Wealth Management Practice* (Shrewsbury, NJ: Charter Financial Publishing Network, 2014).
6. C. Anderson and D. L. Sharpe, "The Efficacy of Life Planning and Communication Tasks in Developing Successful Client-Financial Planner Relationships," *Journal of Financial Planning* 21, no. 6 (2008): 66–77.
7. C. Nelson, "Communication Styles and Business Growth," *Journal of Financial Planning* 23, no. 9 (2010): 8–11.
8. D. Dubofsky and L. Sussman, "The Bonding Continuum in Financial Client-Financial Planner Relationships," *Journal of Financial Planning* 23, no. 10 (2010): 66–78.
9. Id., 76.
10. D. Yeske, "Finding the Planning in Financial Planning."
11. M. Swift and J. Littlechild, "Building Trust through Communication," *Journal of Financial Planning* 28, no. 11 (2015): 28–32.

12. K. C. Harad, "Devise a Client Communication System That Inspires Loyalty," *Journal of Financial Planning* 27, no. 4 (2014): 20–21.
13. T. Christiansen and S. A. DeVaney, "Antecedents of Trust and Commitment in the Financial Client-Financial Planner Relationship," *Journal of Financial Counseling and Planning* 9, no. 2 (1998): 1–10.
14. D. K. Berlo, *The Process of Communication* (New York: International Thomson Publishing, 1960).

Acknowledgments

A book like this does not go from conceptualization to publication without the help of many dedicated people. We would like to thank a number of individuals who helped bring this book project to fruition. To begin with, we are very appreciative for the work and words of Dr. Tom Warschauer, professor emeritus at San Diego State University. It was his question about how a finance faculty member could incorporate communication and counseling skills into a program of study that prompted our first thoughts about writing this book. We are also grateful for those who have helped pave the way for the inclusion of communication topics to be a focus of study in CFP registered programs. A list of everyone who has made an argument for focusing on communication and counseling skills would be too long for this brief dedication, but there are a few who stand out, including: Kristy Archuleta, Elissa Buie, Carol Anderson, Charles Chaffin, Dottie Durband, Bill Gustafson, Sherman Hanna, Rick Kahler, Kevin Keller, Megan Ford, Deana Sharpe, Dave Yeske, and our colleagues at the University of Georgia: Swarn Chatterjee, Jerry Gale, Lance Palmer, Kenneth White, Duncan Williams, Ann Woodyard, and Sheri Worthy. We are also grateful to the leaders at the CFP Board who took a chance in creating the Center for Financial Planning, which provides a forum for works like this that might otherwise never be published.

In the end, this book is dedicated to our financial planning colleagues who are building financial planning into a profession on a daily basis. We know that you are often working alone—sometimes in a firm, a large academic department, or in a small certificate program. It is our hope that this book will be a resource to help you grow your practice or program. If you are an instructor, we hope that the techniques and tools presented in this book help you teach communication and counseling skills more effectively. If you are a student, we hope that you gain practical skills to help you in your career. If you are already a financial planner, our hope is that this small book will help you become even more successful.

On a personal note, we would like to thank our spouses for their unwavering support during the writing process. To Emily, thank you for helping me stay focused on the bigger picture. To Lindsay, I cannot thank you enough for your overall support, and particularly, for taking care of so many important tasks as I dedicated time to this book.

John Grable, PhD, CFP®
and
Joseph Goetz, PhD
Athens, Georgia

How to Use This Book

This book was written with two goals in mind. The first was to help aspiring financial planners develop core competencies related to interpersonal communication techniques. The second was to provide tools and techniques to those already working in the profession to gain mastery of the interpersonal communication process. A key element of the book involves not only reading about "how to communicate," but also watching examples of what to do and what not to do.

Throughout the book you will see text boxes that look like this:

SAMPLE TEXT BOX

Provides title of video relevant to the discussion (for example, Video 4A).

Whenever you see a text box, you should recognize that an accompanying video showing an example of the topic is available online. The text box will provide a code, such as 4A, that will help you find the appropriate video clip. In this example, the number 4 represents the chapter, while the letter A represents the first video in Chapter 4.

While you do not need to watch the videos to gain an understanding, or even a mastery, of the tools and techniques provided in the book, we have found that sometimes watching others do something can be quite informative. We certainly hope that regardless of whether you watch some, all, or none of the videos, you will nonetheless practice what is presented. Mastery comes only with repeated practice.

You can find each of the videos from the book at: www.wiley.com/go/communessentials and enter the password: grable234.

Introduction

The CFP Board Center for Financial Planning is pleased to begin the first in a series of books intended to expand the body of knowledge for financial planning. We envision this series as a platform for discussion for the entire profession, including practitioners, faculty, students, and researchers. We are excited about the opportunity to exchange ideas, validate and challenge assumptions, and help theory inform practice and conversely, practice to inform theory. This series will embody the characteristics of a practitioner-based profession, in which researchers learn from practitioners; practitioners learn from researchers; and ultimately, the profession is even better prepared to help all Americans achieve their financial potential through competent and ethical financial planning.

Although this series is a large step forward, it is not CFP Board's first effort working within the financial planning body of knowledge. For decades, CFP Board has conducted the Job Task Analysis, the largest quantitative study of financial planning practice, to develop a framework for many of the requirements for CFP® certification. CFP Board has also collaborated with hundreds of colleges and universities that house CFP Board Registered Programs, working together to not only meet rigorous curricular standards, but also to enhance student achievement and program sustainability in a variety of institutions, program types, and instructional delivery methods. We also worked together to develop two editions of the *Financial Planning Competency Handbook,* a seminal work that outlines both the breadth of the body of knowledge of financial planning, as well as the interdisciplinary nature of this profession. All of this work, a decades long collaboration and strengthening, is vital to the profession and we look forward to continuing it in the years to come.

We begin the series with *Communication Essentials for Financial Planners: Strategies and Techniques.* We were purposeful in starting with communication, given the importance of client engagement, and all of the actions associated with it, to financial planning practice. Dr. John Grable, CFP® and Dr. Joe Goetz are ideal for this first publication. They both are the embodiment of leaders of a practitioner-based profession: strong researchers who have added relevant theory to the body of knowledge; master educators who have prepared hundreds of current practitioners; and scholars whose work brings tangible impact to financial planning practice. They are respected colleagues and good friends that I have had the pleasure of collaborating with on this important work. I believe this book fills a needed void in the library of financial planning, as it is intended for both future financial planners as well as experienced CFP® professionals both in better engaging the most important element of the financial planning process: the client.

I hope that practitioners who read this book will reflect upon their own client communication and maybe discover ways to perhaps challenge and refine past approaches. Practitioners in a supervisory role may find this book as an effective induction instrument for new hires in their practice. And last, but not least, I hope that students will not only learn some important communication techniques in serving future clients, but also be further motivated to begin a life's work that can be so impactful on the lives of many.

So let us begin our journey together. The intent is not for the reader to passively accept the ideas and theories in this book series. Rather, I hope these books—refined discoveries from the past and incubators for ideas for the future—help practitioners, researchers, educators, and students do their work in making this maturing and evolving profession even better.

Charles R. Chaffin, EdD
Editor

1

An Introduction to Applied Communication

INTRODUCTION

The primary premise of this book is that the financial planning process can be significantly enhanced through the appropriate application of communication theory. By theory, we mean one or more models based on a set of premises that lead to explanations and conclusions. In the preface to this book, we introduced a nine-step framework as a way to conceptualize how financial planners interact with current and prospective clients. A key assumption embedded in this framework is the notion that financial planners who understand and practice the process of communication will be better prepared to help clients reach their financial goals. If you are a student enrolled in a CFP Registered Program, the nine-step process of communication may provide new insights into better ways to communicate with others. If you are already a financial planner, you may find that the framework validates much of what you are currently doing when working with clients. That is, the framework—and communication theory in general—can be used to endorse many of your current practices while providing information to help improve other aspects of interpersonal communication.

Consider the following example. Begin by visualizing a financial planning office. A prospective client makes an appointment to meet with a financial planner. On the day of the meeting, the prospect arrives 10 minutes early. She is seated in the office waiting area. At the appointed time, she is escorted into the financial planner's conference room. A few minutes later the financial planner arrives. She sits down across from the prospect before introducing herself. So far, in this imaginary scene the financial planner has yet to say a word to the prospective client. The question at this point is: Has communication taken place? A novice financial planner might say, "No."

Someone who has more experience probably will say, "Yes." Communication theory would support the experienced financial planner's insight.

Let's evaluate what communication has occurred thus far in this scenario. We know that the prospective client reached out to the financial planner in one way or another to make an appointment. This might have occurred online, through email, or through a phone call. It is also possible that the client made an appointment in person. Regardless of the method, some interaction between the prospect and the financial planner and her staff must have already occurred. This interaction set the stage for further dialog. It is also reasonable to assume that initial conversations laid the groundwork for what the prospect expects from the financial planner. After all, early in the client–financial planner relationship, when a client has only a small amount of information from which to make assumptions, the content of communication is arguably even more important. In general, people tend to overmagnify the meaning of information when only a small amount of information is available. For example, let's assume the prospective client reviewed the financial planner's website, and then initiated a phone call to the planning professional to ask some questions.

> Prospect: "Hello, could you tell me a little about the services you offer."
>
> Planner: "Sure, we provide investment management and retirement planning advice. Would you like to set up an appointment?"
>
> Prospect: "Oh, okay. I guess that would be all right."

At this point, the website and quick phone call served as communication tools to deliver a certain message to the client. What has the financial planner communicated on this short phone call? Did the prospect really want to know about the services offered? Maybe, but maybe she also wanted to know if the people within the firm would be approachable and take the time to listen to her. These *first-impression messages* can be quite powerful and have a lasting effect. Research suggests there may be some truth to the old adage: "You never get a second chance to make a first impression."[1] Given the persistence of first impressions, a financial planner should choose to be intentional in their initial communication with a client.

The financial planner also may benefit from asking open-ended questions to determine what services the client is really looking for and whether the client is a good fit for the services provided by the planner before scheduling an in-person meeting. By asking the right questions, the financial planner may begin building trust and commitment with the client or save time on the part of both the client and financial planner if the relationship is not a good fit.

> Prospect: "Hello, could you tell me a little about the services you offer."
>
> Planner: "Sure, we provide a wide array of financial planning services and customize those services to each client. Perhaps you could help me understand which financial issues you're most interested in addressing.
>
> Prospect: "Oh, okay, well three main concerns come to mind, and they are whether I'm currently saving enough, investing the right way, as well as figuring out a long-term plan for one of my kids who has special needs."
>
> Planner: "Okay, thank you, this information is really helpful. Our team has worked with a number of other families to set up life-care plans for their child who has special needs, as well as provided retirement and investment planning specific to their situation. It sounds like our firm would be a great fit for your needs. Would you like to set up an appointment to learn more about our services?"
>
> Prospect: "Yes, definitely. I'm excited to get started."

Communication between the prospective client and planning staff started again the moment the prospect entered the business premises. Was the person greeted? How was the greeting received? Did the client feel welcomed? Was the prospect immediately offered something to drink or not until she reached the conference room? What were the environmental triggers in the waiting room that signaled the financial planner's working style? Was there a television showing business news or were general readership magazines available to peruse? Was the client sitting in silence? Was there classical music playing in the background, or was the client able to overhear conversations taking place within the office? Each of these elements will be discussed in more detail throughout this book. At this point, it's just important to note that the environment can influence the way clients decode a financial planner's message. The concepts of encoding and decoding a message are examples of elements within communication theory. The office environment and staff interactions, in particular, can shape the manner in which communication does and will take place, as well as influencing the comfort level and expectations of the client.

Now that the client is sitting down directly with the financial planner, imagine that the following brief discussion occurs between the prospect and financial planner:

> Planner: "It is so nice to meet you."
> Prospect: "Thank you for taking the time to meet with me."
> Planner: "You are welcome. How was the traffic today?"
> Prospect: "Not bad. It took only 20 minutes to get here."

It is apparent that some form of communication is occurring. Specifically, the prospective client and financial planner are engaged in *oral discussion*. While communicating orally is very important, there is a lot more to communication than simply talking. Communication encompasses much more than a spoken or written word. Neither the prospective client nor the financial planner are robots speaking in monotones. The way in which the words are spoken and interpreted is just as important—and sometimes more important—than what is actually stated. It is precisely what is not being said that often dictates the manner in which dialog is coded, received, and decoded. That is, what we are not "seeing" in this example are things like:

- Facial expressions
- Tone of voice
- What the financial planner is wearing
- How the prospect and financial planner are seated

We are also not "hearing" how the two are connecting. Would someone interpret the discussion differently if the prospect and financial planner were yelling at each other? Probably so. What if one was whispering and the other was checking emails on a phone. What if the client was trying to make eye contact and the financial planner was mostly looking down or away from the client? Of course, what we do not see or hear in this example is just as important as what we know has occurred.

The purpose of this chapter is to set the groundwork for improving the communication skills and competencies of financial planners. Our approach in this chapter involves outlining the most relevant *theories of communication* in an effort to help readers both understand and apply communication techniques to meet a key learning objective as outlined by the Certified Financial Planner Board of Standards Inc. (CFP Board).

FINANCIAL PLANNING OUTCOMES

The CFP Board is the primary academic oversight body for colleges and universities that provide financial planner education at the undergraduate, graduate, and certificate levels in the United States. The CFP Board also provides oversight to the more than 75,000 U.S.-based CFP professionals who practice on a daily basis. Currently, the CFP Board has identified 72 financial planning topics that all registered programs must include at an advanced level when providing education and training to students. By definition, it is assumed that all practicing financial planners are familiar with and competent in the application of these learning outcomes. Of particular importance are the learning outcomes in topic B.15 as described in the CFP Board's *Student-Centered Learning Objectives Based upon CFP Board Principal Topics*[2]:

Principles of Communication and Counseling
1. Explain the applications of counseling theory to financial planning practice
2. Demonstrate how a planner can develop a relationship of honesty and trust in client interaction
3. Assess the components of communications, including linguistic signs and nonverbal communications
4. Apply active listening skills when communicating with clients
5. Select appropriate counseling and communication techniques for use with individual clients

This book provides readers with tools and techniques, in written form, graphically, and through audiovisual formats, to achieve these outcomes. In order to address these outcomes, it is first important to define exactly what we mean by *communication*.

COMMUNICATION DEFINED

What is *communication*? Despite the simplicity of this question, the answer is somewhat elusive. In fact, there are hundreds of definitions floating through academia that attempt to address this query. Some argue that communication is the act of transmitting a message from a sender to a receiver.[3] Within this definitional framework, the receiver can be conceptualized quite broadly, from one person to millions of people. Others have argued that communication is the process of interacting through messaging.[4] Heath and Bryant noted that communication can be viewed as a process of on-going events—either intentional or random—that result in conversations or encounters.[5] While none of the hundreds of communication definitions are entirely satisfactory, we recommend adopting a view of communication as being primarily process driven. For financial planners, this perspective may make the most intuitive sense. The process, which is described in more detail later in the chapter, entails the creation and sharing of information to enhance mutual understanding.[6]

This working definitional framework highlights two important elements of communication. First, communication is sensual. By this we mean that communication requires at least one of the five senses, such as sight or hearing. Both are essential to the transmittal and receipt of communicated messages. However, it is also possible that the senses of touch, smell, and taste can aid someone's ability to communicate. Consider situations when someone has touched you. A handshake can be a warm welcome or a luke-warm reception. If the touch was meant as a welcoming measure, the sensation might enhance communication. If, on the other hand, the experience is negative, the result can be a discussion with elevated levels of tension. There is a powerful element of perception involved here. The perception of the client relative to the success of the communication channel(s) is paramount. Each client's perceptions will be different. Additionally, every financial planner's reactions will be different.

Second, communication is a learned activity. Obtaining the skills necessary to communicate and to interpret communication properly is required to successfully establish and maintain professional relationships. This means that communication is as much about the context of dialog as it is about the word or pictures used. Consider the often-used phrase "you guys." Today, it is quite common for speakers to address an audience by saying something like, "How are you guys doing?" As audience members we have learned that this blatantly sexist phrase is meant as a generalized welcome statement, not a term to inflame gender bias. Yet, this is only true within the context of American lexicon. In other words, we have learned to hear the words "you guys" and immediately interpret the meaning as gender neutral.

Within the environment of financial planning, it is hoped that communication will be intentional. That is, communicating with clients, colleagues, staff, and others should be related to a specific purpose. That purpose may be to:

- Establish a working relationship
- Develop trust
- Obtain information

- Create boundaries
- Persuade others to do something
- Facilitate decision making
- Exert power

Purposeful communication can be a form of self-expression. We know, for example, a faculty member at a major university who wears only multicolored sneakers and T-shirts to work. Although we do not recommend this form of nonverbal communication to students studying financial planning because it conveys an image of casualness, we certainly admire our colleague's creative self-expression. Our colleague, whether intentional or not, is communicating a number of personal and environmental cues merely by the manner in which she is dressed. Keep this in mind: generally, unintentional communication is something to be avoided, especially within the context of a client–financial planner relationship. For example, we have another colleague who has a very indirect way of asking questions. In fact, he starts nearly every discussion with a question that is neither rhetorical nor easily answered. The result is generally a dialog that loses focus and creates conflict. The funny thing is that he does this unintentionally, and often wonders why others do not invite him to lunch or to meetings.

It is also important, before moving deeper into the book, to further delineate what we mean by communication. As shown in Figure 1.1, there are four general *categories of communication*[7]: (1) intrapersonal, (2) interpersonal, (3) group, and (4) mass.

Intrapersonal communication refers to the dialogs we all have in our own minds. Sometimes we argue with ourselves, while at other times we daydream

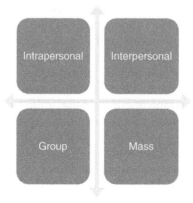

FIGURE 1.1   Categories of Communication

about faraway adventures. *Interpersonal communication,* on the other hand, deals with communication between two people or sometimes within small structured units (for example, families). *Group communication,* as the name implies, involves communication within and to larger groups of people. *Mass communication* involves messaging to very large groups, typically through electronic channels. Of the categories of communication, mastering mass communication is the least valuable in regard to building a successful financial planning practice. Within academia, the majority of those with a doctorate in communication studies deal with mass communication issues.

While each category of communication is certainly important within the context of financial planning, we are primarily interested in exploring *interpersonal communication* strategies, tools, and techniques. Financial planning, as a professional endeavor, is premised on the notion of one person helping another person, family, or entity. Financial planning is, at its core, a helping profession. To be effective as help providers, financial planners must possess an interest in improving their communication skills. Not only must financial planners acquire communication skills, but they also need to practice communicating reflectively and reflexively. These terms were introduced by Donald Schon[8] in 1983. Schon argued that professionals have an obligation to reflect on the effectiveness and correctness of their thoughts and conceptualizations of reality. Schon argued that rather than be satisfied with the way you are doing something today, improvement can occur continuously by consciously evaluating emotions, experiences, actions, and responses. This evaluation is two-pronged. First, it is important to evaluate how you are feeling and reacting. Second, it is imperative that you empathize with those around you. This means accounting for the emotions and reactions of colleagues and clients, synthesizing these reactions, and changing behavior accordingly.

When viewed from the concept of reflective practice, the ability to communicate effectively is the most important factor in determining a financial planner's success. Some might argue that technical skills related to financial projections, the ability to create and manage portfolios, or the capability to develop complex asset protection models are what make great financial planners. This might, in fact, be true. However, we would argue that financial planning aptitude alone is not enough to guarantee success within the profession. More important, in our thinking, is the competence to effectively deliver the message of financial planning to prospective and current clients. Think of it this way: the majority of clients are looking for advice from a dependable professional. They want to engage the services of someone they can trust. *Trust,* for better or worse, is shaped in large part by client perceptions of the financial planner's skills and abilities. *Perception* is, in turn, formed most directly through communication technique. This relationship is shown in Figure 1.2.

FIGURE 1.2   The Process of Building Trust

Financial planners who are functionally competent, but lack the skills to communicate their competence, will always be at a competitive disadvantage when compared to financial planners who are skilled in both the planning process and communicating outcomes of the process.

THE THEORY OF COMMUNICATION

Consider again the definitions of communication from our earlier discussion. A key assumption embedded in each definition is that communication is a process. Specifically, communication involves the transmittal and receipt of information and ideas from one person or group to another. More importantly, the process can be interpreted only if the context of conversation is known.

Quickly scan Figure 1.3. What is occurring here? Without knowing the context of the discussion, it is easy to imagine any number of scenarios. Look at the girl's face. Is she responding to a request or about to pose a question?

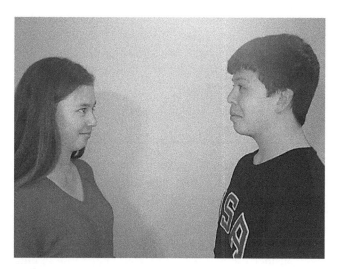

FIGURE 1.3   Interpreting the Context of Conversation

Is the young man standing impassively or is he engaged in active listening? Maybe something else entirely has happened. Without some understanding of the context surrounding a conversation, it is often impossible to fully grasp the purpose of communication.

Figure 1.3 also illustrates the five elements necessary for communication to occur. According to Dimbleby and Burton,[9] the *process of communication* must include a:

1. Sender
2. Message
3. Form
4. Receiver
5. Effect

In Figure 1.3, for example, let's assume that the young man shared an idea with the girl. Using the process of communication from before, he was the *sender*. The *message* is the idea or information shared. We do not know by looking at the picture what the message was. *Form* refers to the method of communication or what was described previously as the channel of communication. In this situation, oral dialog is the form of communication. Other forms of communication include writing, singing, dancing, and using sign language, to name just a few. The girl in Figure 1.3 is the *receiver* of the message. *Effect* refers to the receipt and interpretation of the message, or what was described as decoding in the Financial Planning Communication and Counseling Skills Framework described earlier. Apparently, the girl has received the message, and based solely on her facial expression and body position (that is, leaning away from the sender), the young man's thought has had an effect. It is important to remember, however, that without an understanding of the context of communication, it is not truly possible to know if the effect was positive or negative.

THE IMPORTANCE OF FEEDBACK

While the five elements of communication conceptually define the process of interaction, the system of dialog described earlier lacks another essential element; namely, *feedback*. To understand the meaning of feedback, we must first delve more deeply into the theory of communication.

At its most basic level, *language* is composed of nothing more than a series of *signs*. Writing is the best example of communication as a grouping of signs. Consider the words on this page. For those familiar with the English language, the lines, dashes, curves, and dots on this page make sense.

That is, the context of sentences and paragraphs, made up of generally recognized signs, can be interpreted by most anyone familiar with the English language. What happens when someone who speaks and reads only English visits another country, such as South Korea? The Koreans created a very functional writing system thousands of years ago called *Hangugeo* (한국어). Korean script is interesting to look at and is easily interpreted by those familiar with the language. The average American visiting Seoul, however, would have a difficult, if not impossible, time communicating with native Koreans using only Korean script. While the American may recognize the signs of writing, the knowledge (remember that communication is a learned skill) to communicate effectively will generally be missing.

Verbal communication is also composed primarily of signs. Think of signs as additional communication context. Consider the following discussion:

> Ted: "Jim, how did you like the boss's speech today?"
>
> Jim: "Well, the boss made some really interesting points."
>
> Ted: "He sure did. The one about following in his footsteps by working harder really made me think."

This example shows how easy it is to misinterpret a message if the signs of communication are not agreed upon or understood. As outsiders reading the transcript of the dialog, we might conclude that both Ted and Jim have deep admiration for their boss. Based only on the signs shown in the callout (that is, the words alone) this would be a logical conclusion. However, what we do not see is the way the message was encoded. That is, it is very unlikely that Ted transmitted his words in a shallow monotone voice. Equally unlikely is the prospect that Jim received the words at face value. Instead, he decoded the words, taking into account the manner in which Ted conveyed his message.

This highlights a critical aspect of effective communication. Both the sender and receiver must understand the signs being used. A precondition of effective communication is that the receiver be able to decode and interpret the signs quickly. In some ways, this sounds like a complex game of spy-versus-spy. While not strictly accurate, there are elements of truth in the analogy. Communication tends to be culturally specific. Americans, for example, use signs that are different from communication signs employed in other cultures. It takes time to learn about specific communication signs and signals. It takes even longer to acquire the skills necessary to decode messages. This helps explain why we tend to laugh at characters in movies who try to speak a nonnative language to someone fluent in another language. By definition, the nonnative speaker will almost always misinterpret signs of communication.

Let's revisit the dialog between Ted and Jim. This time, notice the inclusion of encoded signs sent by both men. The italicized dialog represents the intrapersonal decoding of the original message:

Ted (slapping Jim on the shoulder): "Jim, how did you like the boss's speech today?"

Decoded: "Ted is about to share something on a personal level."

Jim (shrugging his shoulders): "Well, the boss made some really interesting points."

Decoded: "Jim does not want to say anything until he knows where this conversation is going."

Ted (almost laughing): "He sure did (wink). The one about following in his footsteps by working harder really made me think."

Decoded: "Got it. Ted thinks our boss is a hypocrite."

Readers whose native language is English will almost certainly interpret this revised dialog as being based on sarcasm. It is unlikely that either Ted or Jim hold their boss in high esteem. We know this because Ted has encoded his serious words with humor. Jim was able to decode the message as being ironic. Ted went further and included a wink (a physical sign) to ensure that Jim really understood that he was making fun of his boss. While Ted's words would never betray his contempt for the boss's speech, the way the message was encoded certainly indicates a lack of respect.

To interpret communication signs, it is necessary to have the correct *deciphering codes*. Codes help a person interpret the true meaning of a message. Think of Morse code. This form of communication is based on electronic dot and dash signals. The combination of dots and dashes make up letters, which can then be combined into words and sentences. Anyone who understands the coding associated with the Morse system can communicate with others who also understand the code. American Sign Language is another example of how signs and codes are interrelated. Each hand movement represents a specific letter or word. For those who understand the coding structure, American Sign Language can open up additional doors of communication.

This returns us to the concept of feedback. In the simple model of communication, as described earlier in the chapter, we said that effective communication requires a sender, message, form or channel, receiver, and effect. To this model we added the concepts of encoding and decoding. This evolving model was framed by the context of shared information. Implicit within this discussion is the concept of feedback. As the dialog between Ted and Jim illustrates, communication involves a give and take between sender and receiver. For those familiar with a particular language, there are certain *rules* that should be followed. It is these rules that provide a framework for decoding messages. Think about subcultures within American society. In some cities, for example, it is unwise to wear hats, shirts, and jackets that show the logos of some professional sports teams. Within these communities, certain logos have been adopted as signs to communicate allegiance to street gangs. Wearing one of these logos may break an unspoken social rule by communicating disrespect for gang members.

As two people engage in dialog, they are actively—even if unconsciously—decoding the other person's message. *Decoding* entails interpretation of the words, gestures, facial expressions, and other unspoken characteristics embedded in the dialog. As shown in Figure 1.4, this becomes a very quickly evolving circular process in which messages are sent, received, and decoded. Almost always, some type of response is returned. This is the essence of feedback. Stated another way, the sender becomes the receiver, and vice versa, with each person in the dialog coding, decoding, interpreting, and responding to messages.

Remember, a response need not be verbal. Think back to the picture of the two young people engaged in dialog. The young girl's face says as much as the words she might speak. Feedback helps those engaged in dialog

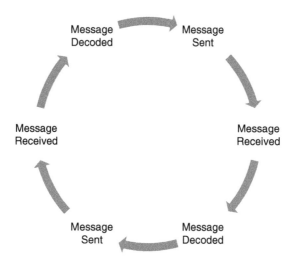

FIGURE 1.4 Circular Process of Messaging and Decoding

determine if more information is needed, if the pace of discussion needs to be quickened or reduced, or whether the discussion can be terminated. Feedback can also be quite useful in helping an observant communicator determine whether their message is being received and interpreted appropriately.

It is this last point that provides the foundation for the remainder of this book. *A primary role of a financial planner is to provide information to clients in such a way that a client is willing to take action.* The action may be implementing a recommendation, agreeing to additional planning work, or referring someone to work with the financial planner. Feedback from a client is the primary way in which a financial planner will know if his or her words and behaviors are making sense. The good news is this: clients may not know it, but they are constantly decoding a financial planner's messages and sending feedback that can be interpreted and directed. Financial planners who understand how to code messages effectively and interpret feedback will be in a better position when it comes to helping their clients reach the client's financial objectives and goals.

Figure 1.5 illustrates a simplified model of the Financial Planning Communication and Counseling Skills Framework presented earlier in the book. The

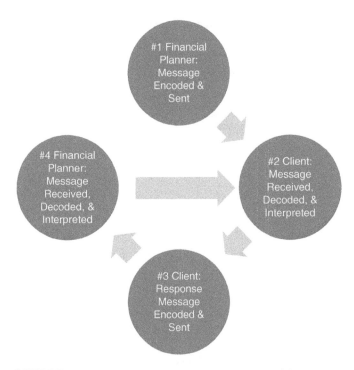

FIGURE 1.5   Financial Planning Communication Model

model encompasses the elements of a sender and receiver and the coding and decoding of messages. The arrows linking the functional boxes represent both direction of communication and feedback within the communication process. The circular and fast-moving aspect of communication creates a situation in which the direction of communication becomes quite complex. The receiver of a message will automatically begin decoding the moment a verbal or nonverbal cue is presented. This, in turn, creates feedback for the person who is sending the message. Remember too that the receipt of feedback results in a reaction to the other person. That is, both financial planner and client are actively engaged in interpreting the words and mannerisms of each other, within the context of the financial planning engagement. This information is used by both parties to shape future messages. The expected outcome effect of the communication process is an enhanced client–financial planner relationship.

CONCLUSION

Aspiring financial planners are sometimes amazed that the concept of communication can be so complicated. Even experienced planners are sometimes caught off-guard as to how regular communication might be interpreted in a variety of different and unexpected ways. On the one hand, what seems like a natural day-to-day activity, such as talking to a client or colleague, seems like something anyone should naturally be able to do. On the other hand, after reading this chapter, this notion should be seen for what it is—a myth. Communication is a learned process and skill that can always be further developed.

No one is born a great communicator. Expert communication must be learned and practiced, just like any other skill. Rather than viewing communication as simply an interpersonal conversation between two or more people, we argue that communication is really a process whereby senders and receivers share signs. These signs must be interpreted through the use of mutually accepted codes. Effective communication occurs only when messages are coded correctly, decoded successfully, and interpreted efficiently. The remainder of this book is devoted to identifying some of the most important interpersonal forms of verbal and nonverbal communication that can be used by financial planners to improve the work with clients when following the financial planning process.

SUMMARY

Before starting down this path of communication exploration, let's revisit the young woman and man from earlier in the chapter. Is it possible, after reading this chapter, to glean more information from Figure 1.6? In the

FIGURE 1.6   Communication Interpretation

interest of full disclosure, one of these two young people is one of the author's teenage children. Here is how the picture can be interpreted:

1. The young man is the sender of a message.
2. The young woman is the receiver.
3. Their form of communication is verbal.
4. They are both using words, eye contact, and body positions as signs within the conversation.
5. The context of the conversation follows one of Dad's instructions— "Tell your sister a funny joke."
6. The young man's words were coded with humor.
7. She was able to decode the words through a shared understanding of what is considered funny within the family.
8. Her smile provides feedback that the joke was received and decoded effectively; the joke was interpreted as effective.
9. His smile is a form of nonverbal feedback to her that he appreciates others in the family knowing the brilliance of his wit.
10. The end of the communication process is an increase in experience on the part of the young man; he is now more confident is his joke-telling abilities.
11. She leaves the conversation in a better mood with the knowledge of a good joke to tell her friends.

CHAPTER APPLICATIONS

1. Communication refers to the
   I. Creation and sharing of information
   II. Process of enhancing mutual understanding
   III. Exclusive use of interpersonal dialog
      a. I only
      b. III only
      c. I and II only
      d. I, II, and III

2. Mannerisms, such as winking, frowning, and laughing, represent what within the communication process?
   a. Signs
   b. Codes
   c. Interpretations
   d. Outcomes

3. When viewed from a financial planning perspective, which of the following categories of communication is of least importance for an individual practitioner?
   a. Intrapersonal
   b. Interpersonal
   c. Group
   d. Mass

4. Communication must include all of the following, except:
   a. A message
   b. An effect
   c. An interpreter
   d. A form

5. Feedback refers to
   a. The ability to decode a message
   b. A response returned from a receiver to a message sender
   c. The quickening of discussion
   d. A situation in which discussion becomes complex

6. _____ entails interpretation of the words, gestures, facial expressions, and other unspoken characteristics embedded in the dialog
   a. Contextualizing
   b. Decoding
   c. Responding
   d. Sending

7. All of the following are true regarding the elements of communication, except:
   a. Communication is sensual.
   b. Communication requires the use of codes.
   c. Communication is purposeful.
   d. Communication always entails feedback.

8. Which of the following should be minimized, if not avoided, when communicating with clients?
   a. Unintentional communication
   b. Intrapersonal communication
   c. Intentional communication
   d. Purposeful communication

9. Which of the following associations is correct?
   a. Signs of communication must be interpreted through the mutually accepted codes.
   b. Codes must be interpreted from encoded signs.
   c. Intrapersonal conversation must precede interpersonal communication.
   d. All of the above are true.

10. Nedra would like to send a group email to her office staff. Which of the following tasks comes first in the communication process?
    a. Interpreting message content
    b. Responding to potential negative nonverbal feedback
    c. Encoding the message
    d. Sending the message

11. Find a partner (this could be a colleague or classmate). Stand in front of each other and attempt to carry on a conversation without the use of verbal or nonverbal coding. This means talking in a monotone voice without physical expression. How long were you able to keep up the conversation? How did it make you feel when your ability to decode a message was severely limited? Finally, how did your partner feel listening and responding to you?

12. Choose a new partner. This time, engage in a similar discussion but attempt to be as animated as possible. Raise your voice and use as much body language (for example, moving the arms, leaning toward and away from your partner, and so on) as reasonable. How did this make you feel, especially in comparison to the first exercise? How long were you able to keep the conversation going? How do you think your partner felt listening and responding to you?

13. Turn on a reality television show. Be sure to mute the volume. Is it possible to interpret what is happening on the show just from the nonverbal signs and mannerisms shown? Do you think someone who does not speak English, or is not familiar with American culture, would be able to do a better or worse job of interpretation? Why or why not?

14. Consider whether your nonverbal coding or body language is ever inconsistent with the messages you are encoding or trying to send and make a list of these tendencies. For example, some the financial planning students who work in the authors' campus-based financial planning clinic have a tendency to smile or smirk when they are nervous or don't know how to respond to a highly negative and emotional statement from a client. Could this create a breakdown in the communication between the sender and receiver? Many people have these incongruent communication tendencies. It is important that you are aware of them and address them with clients to prevent misinterpretation.

NOTES

1. B. Gawronski, R. J. Rydell, B. Vervliet, and J. De Houwer, "Generalization versus Contextualization in Automatic Evaluation," *Journal of Experimental Psychology: General* 139, no. 4 (2010): 683–701. doi: 10.1037/a0020315.
2. Resource Document available at: www.cfp.net/downloads/CFPBoard_Learning_Objectives_Resource_2012-08.pdf.
3. J. A. Devito, *The Communication Handbook: A Dictionary* (New York: Harper & Row, 1986).
4. G. Gerbner, "An Institutional Approach to Mass Communication Research," in *Communication: Theory and Research*, ed. L. Thayer (Springfield, IL: Charles C. Thomas, 1967), 429–445.
5. R. L. Heath and J. Bryant, *Human Communication Theory and Research* (Hillsdale, NJ: Lawrence Erlbaum Associates, 2000).
6. E. M. Rogers and D. L. Kincaid, *Communication Networks: Toward a New Paradigm for Research* (New York: Free Press, 1981).
7. R. Dimbleby and G. Burton, *More Than Words: An Introduction to Communication* (New York: Methuen, 1985).
8. D. A. Schon, *The Reflective Practitioner: How Professionals Think in Action* (New York: Basic Books, 1983).
9. Id., 22.

2

Structuring the Process of Interpersonal Communication

INTRODUCTION

As mentioned in the previous chapter, the focus of this book is squarely in the category of interpersonal communication. Although this topic may seem straightforward, this area of communication can get quite complex. There are several important assumptions and concepts that frame the ideas and expected outcomes related to client–financial planner communication interactions. We are going to look at these elements of interpersonal communication in detail.

This chapter introduces some theoretical concepts to help describe what happens when a client and financial planner engage in communication. Don't let the term "theoretical" worry you. A *theory* is a tool that helps explain or predict some phenomenon. Think about Einstein's theory of relativity. This theory was developed to explain how mass and energy are related. Today, $E = mc^2$ is part of the common scientific lexicon. One hundred and fifty years ago, however, this concept did not exist. Einstein's theory has been rigorously tested. These tests ultimately led to the theory's wide acceptance as a framework for explaining and predicting cosmic events. While we are not about to compare our exploration of communication techniques and tools to the importance of explaining the space/time continuum, we are, nonetheless, going to focus on concepts that best explain how effective communication occurs.

Given the focus of this book, we need to start by determining what is meant by the phrase "interpersonal communication?" Heath and Bryant[1] defined the phrase as follows:

> *Interpersonal communication* is dyadic interaction in which people negotiate relationships by using communication styles and strategies that become personally meaningful as the persons involved attempt

to reduce uncertainty (about themselves, their partners, and their relationships), to be self-efficacious, and to maximize rewards through interactions.

This definition implies the following things:

- First, interpersonal communication is relationship driven. That is, financial planners and their clients work in a world in which what is done or said has a direct impact on the other person. Communication affects both the client and the financial planner, not just the client. If effective, communication can prompt attitudinal and behavioral change. Through reflection-in-action and reflection-on-action, for example, a financial planner can alter his or her approach when engaged in client interactions. This can occur when a financial planner pays attention to what he or she is saying and how the client is responding. This reflective practice can then be used to help a client better understand the motivation behind a planner's words and recommendations.
- Second, communication goes well beyond the content of a message. Those who are engaged in interpersonal communication are always, to some extent, interpreting content, context, and the effect of what is said or done. This is true for financial planners and clients. Sometimes, the evaluation is a haphazard affair. At other times, the evaluation can be reflective of words and actions. When this occurs, either by the financial planner or the client, communication enters a deeper, more meaningful level.
- Third, people tend to engage in ongoing communication only when the benefits of doing so outweigh the costs.

This last point is of particular importance when assessed from the perspective of financial planning. Clients will tend to stay engaged in the planning process if they believe that the benefits associated with financial planning outweigh the costs. At the initial stages of the financial planning process, clients can best gauge the cost and benefit of a relationship through interpersonal discussions with their financial planner. Rather than viewing costs strictly from a cash flow and net worth perspective, it is important to note that clients also view relationship costs as a factor in determining whether to move forward with financial planning. When interpersonal communication is seen as the primary element driving the perception of costs and benefits, it becomes apparent that financial planners who are skilled communicators have an advantage over others because they are in a better position to present their value proposition in a way that reduces "costs" while maximizing "benefits" for clients.

SOCIAL PENETRATION THEORY

The vitality of any relationship is based on the quality of communication. This is the underlying premise of social penetration theory. This theory was developed by Altman and Taylor[2] in the early 1970s. They argued that relationships follow a common pattern that mirrors conversation. A key assumption within the theory is that people initially project an outward image that they hope will influence others. This image may or may not be a true representation of the person.

Some individuals play roles that they believe enhance their social position. Financial planners encounter this on a daily basis. It is quite common for men, in particular, to respond superficially to questions regarding investment risk tolerance. In modern society, men often positively correlate strength and power with risk taking. So, to ask a man how risk tolerant he is in relation to financial risk often produces answers that have no basis in reality. Stated another way, men tend to overestimate and report their willingness to take on financial risk. Women, on the other hand, sometimes underestimate their tolerance for risk. They sometimes do this to appear less financially savvy than they actually are as a way to elicit basic financial information from their financial planner. Sometimes women just undervalue their financial knowledge and insights, and as such, they undermine their own financial risk-taking attributes. This initial outward image is often not an accurate portrayal of the client's true attitude or preference.

Deception is not just a gender-related issue. Some people are prone to exhibit signs of wealth that exceed their true financial position. A financial planner is best advised to confirm that someone who engages in conspicuous consumption (for example, wears designer clothes, drives expensive cars, and lives in an expensive house) actually has the wherewithal to match their outward appearance. This is difficult to do during an initial meeting with a prospective client and without a high quality of communication.

Beyond these specific examples, it is quite natural for clients to engage in some level of impression management or self-presentation that is overly positive when first meeting their financial planner. Unfortunately, this social desirability bias may discourage the disclosure of past financial decisions, debt levels, or financial conflicts with a partner or spouse—all of which are very valuable for the financial planner to know. Thus, improving the quality of communication, and in turn, the relationship as quickly as possible is quite valuable to the financial planning process. According to social penetration theory, relationships, and the way financial planners and clients communicate, go through four distinct stages. These stages mirror the manner in which relationships are formed and developed:

1. Orientation
2. Exploration
3. Affective (emotional) exchanges
4. Stability

The linear progression of the communication process is illustrated in Figure 2.1. These stages can best be differentiated when contextualized according to the level of intimacy and disclosure that occurs. The word *penetration* was adopted by Taylor and Altman to describe how the senders and receivers of messages must break through to deeper levels of intimacy and disclosure for a relationship to grow and become stronger, which can occur over varying times.

ORIENTATION

Consider a typical initial meeting between a financial planner and a prospective client. The financial planner has a limited amount of time to meet, greet, and obtain key information from the prospect. The prospective client, on the other hand, may also have time constraints. More importantly, he or she may be unsure if he or she is willing to work with the financial planner or engage in the planning process.

At this stage of the relationship, both parties are primarily interested in learning more about each other. It is also true that both the financial planner and the client may be displaying characteristics that are intended to either mask some information or to present an image that will persuade the other person in some manner or form. The financial planner, for example, may stage the meeting in a luxurious conference room as a way to communicate wealth, success, and stability to the prospect. The prospective client may do the same thing. He or she may wear an expensive watch or ring to signify that he or she has the wealth necessary to work with the financial planner.

FIGURE 2.1   The Linear Stages of Client–Financial Planner Communication

It is common at this stage of the communication process for the level of intimacy and disclosure to be marked by cautiousness and generalities. In some respects, the level of conversation may be superficial, with the client unwilling to share detailed information or facts that he or she thinks may be interpreted negatively by the financial planner. Conversational phrases such as, "It is very nice to meet you," "How was the traffic," and "May I get you something to drink" are examples of orienting questions.

The orientation stage of communication is used as a way for both parties to evaluate the future value of the relationship. In some ways, this is just like the dating scene. When two people come together for the first time, they most often engage in low-level chitchat with the intent of finding common ground or a connection. Communication experts call this intrapersonal communication analytics. The process of evaluation, based on verbal and nonverbal cues, is done primarily automatically and unconsciously. Each person is involved in subjectively evaluating the competence, sincerity, and trustworthiness of the other person. If a connection is made, the conversation will move to the exploration stage.

The time frame involved from moving from one stage to the other is based entirely on how well the financial planner and prospective client connect with each other. This potential connection is based on myriad factors, including levels of trust, likeability, and perceived ability to meet one's needs. Later in this chapter we discuss explicitly how clients, and sometimes financial planners, make the decision to move forward with developing a relationship. Suffice it to say, there is a strong likelihood that prospective clients will move from orientation to exploration relatively quickly—within the initial meeting or in a second meeting—if they intend to work with a financial planner. If the decision is made to exit the relationship, this, too, will happen quickly.

EXPLORATION

Explorative communication is concerned primarily with prompting and uncovering deep, more penetrating, revelations. At this stage of communication, the participants move away from cautious remarks to exchanges based on emotions, feelings, concerns, and desires. While the content of discussion may be serious, the manner of conversation is generally more relaxed and friendly. In other words, both the financial planner and the client (this assumes the prospective client moves from exploration to engagement) have shared enough information to promote further disclosure. Here is an example of an explorative dialog:

> Planner: "So, you have been saving a portion of your paycheck into your company's 401(k) plan every month. Is that correct?"
>
> Client: "Yes."
>
> Planner: "How has the 401(k) been performing?"
>
> Client: "Not so good. Since I started, I think my average return has been something like 4 percent annually."
>
> Planner: "How does that make you feel?"
>
> Client: "Terrible! I am worried that I won't have enough money for retirement."

As this example illustrates, an exploratory exchange involves a deeper revelation of information compared to orientation dialog. Even so, a financial planner needs additional information to build a deeper relationship with the client. Stated another way, the communication exchange must continue to advance.

AFFECTIVE EXCHANGE

While exploratory exchanges allow a client to reveal more information through disclosure, affective exchange goes one step further. During this stage of communication, the client is not only willing to disclose information but may also hope to strengthen the client–financial planner relationship through bonds of friendship.

In some respects, the affective exchange phase of the communication process is a continuation of the exploration phase. The financial planner and client now know much more about each other, both professionally and personally. Financial planners who work with clients at this stage of a relationship may begin most conversations with a brief inquiry about the client's family, health, and other personal interests. Rather than being a tool of exploration, affective exchange is designed to elicit true feelings and emotions. Affective exchange further cements bonds of trust, open disclosure, sincerity, and intimacy. Statements such as, "I truly value your opinion" or "You always have a unique way of saying things that make sense to me" represent clues that a client views the relationship in terms of affective exchange. Reaching the affective exchange phase of communication is important because it allows the financial planning professional to fully understand the goals of the client, as it provides a level of comfort to the client that encourages the sharing of what is truly most important to him or her.

STABLE EXCHANGE

Relationships that continue to blossom often move into a stable pattern. Communication that occurs at this stage of the communication process is open, free flowing, and generally unconstrained. *Stability* is characterized by exchanges during conversation that are marked by open, frank, and intimate sharing of information, ideas, and strategies. Clients know their financial planner very well at this stage. Financial planners, likewise, have both a clinical and personal feel for their clients. They are generally able to anticipate questions, feelings, and behavioral tendencies. Conversations tend to be open, friendly, and meaningful. Here is an example of a stable exchange:

Client: "Lance, what do you think is the long-term trend in silver prices?"

Planner: "Why do you ask?"

Client: "I'm thinking of buying some shares in a silver ETF."

Planner: "Come on now, you know we have already discussed precious metal investing."

Client: "I know, but I heard some good news on the television today. The guy on TV said silver was going higher."

Planner: "Mike, you kill me sometimes. How many times have I told you to stop watching those shows? The financial news shows you're watching are nothing more than sensationalism and propaganda. Give it a rest and forget silver ETFs."

Client: "Yah, I suppose you're right. You usually are. Kind of a stupid idea, but I thought I'd ask anyway. Hey, do you want to grab some lunch?"

How often would a discussion like this occur during a meeting between a financial planner and a prospective client? Not very often, if ever. This level of discussion, with high disclosure and relationship intimacy, can generally only happen once a financial planner and client have full trust in each other. This typically occurs only during times of conversational and relationship stability. In this case, the planner is familiar with the client's speaking style and what specifically resonates with Lance. It is all about working within the clients' comfort zone and the strength of the relationship.

It is important to remember, however, that not all relationships move quickly or fully from orientation to stability. Sometimes a relationship will be characterized only by orientation exchanges, which will then result in a dissolution of the relationship (that is, the financial planner and client go

different ways). Other relationships may linger in an exploratory communication phase. When this occurs, a financial planner will likely conclude that
the client is procrastinating. While there may be trust within the relationship, the level of intimacy to create a long-lasting bond between the client
and the financial planner may be missing. What is needed, according to most
communication experts, is a linear transformation from orientation to affect
and stability. This is the key to establishing a trusting and committed professional relationship, which is characterized by a bond of open sharing,
disclosure, and intimacy.

RELATIONSHIP BENEFITS AND COSTS

Readers who accept the notion that interpersonal communication is a process with distinct stages of sharing almost always ask how a financial planner or client decides to keep progressing in the relationship. That is to say,
how does one decide to move from a level of exploratory exchange to affective or stable exchange? The answer to this question is surprisingly simple.
Individuals, as economic hypotheses indicate, generally make relationship
decisions on the basis of costs versus benefits. This weighing of costs and
benefits is sometimes done explicitly but almost always implicitly. Taylor
and Altman[3] summarized the cost/benefit tradeoff choices people make with
the following formula[4]:

Assessment of Relationship = Relationship Rewards – Relationship Costs

This formula implies the following:

Decision to Remain in Relationship
= Relationship Rewards > Relationship Costs

or

Decision to Terminate Relationship
= Relationship Rewards < Relationship Costs

What are the benefits and costs inherent in a financial planning relationship? To find the answer, it is first important to understand a key assumption underlying social penetration theory. Taylor and Altman argued that
the growth of a relationship from orientation to stability does not occur
without some hardship and struggle. It is precisely how a financial planner

and client evaluate rewards that determine how a relationship crisis is dealt with. Obvious rewards for a client include increased financial knowledge, confidence, peace of mind, and wealth. Costs include money, time, and effort. Financial planners also receive benefits from engaging with clients, such as increased income, satisfaction, and prestige. Financial planner costs include time, effort, and lost opportunities to work with other prospective clients.

What is most important to remember, however, is that the relationship itself can be viewed as both a cost and a benefit. It is possible for a financial planner to enthusiastically look forward to meeting with a client, even though the client's assets under management or financial capacity may be quite limited. Stated another way, the financial planner might find the relationship itself to be rewarding. Maybe the client provides intellectual stimulation, or the financial planner may find that the client is truly benefiting from the advice given. This may provide the financial planner with an intrinsic sense of value. Another low-net-worth client may be of large financial value to a firm by way of being a center of influence who refers many high-net-worth clients. A young professional may not have any investable assets but be of great benefit to the firm through providing specific training opportunities with mitigated risk. Imagine allowing a young financial planner, who just graduated, to take the lead in the case and in client meetings, thereby accelerating his or her professional development and value to the firm.

Clients, on the other hand, may find the client–financial planner relationship to be costly. It makes no difference if the financial planner sees things differently. Maybe the client finds the financial planner's personality to be abrasive or maybe he or she feels another adviser can generate a higher rate of return. If, at some point, the client evaluates the financial planner's personality, portfolio management, or comprehensive financial planning to be more costly than the value of advice received, the client will likely terminate the relationship.

Clients, as well as financial planners, also engage in *cost forecasting*. They take what is being said and done in one meeting and use this information to forecast the long-term benefits and costs associated with the relationship. Consider a situation in which a financial planner is meeting with a client for, say, the third time. The issues being discussed may be the same as during the first two meetings. The financial planner may be expecting the client to take action, and finding no action taken, conclude that the client is either unable or unwilling to implement suggestions. Using this experience, the financial planner will be apt to forecast similar behavior from the client in the future. Given this scenario, the financial planner may conclude that it is best to terminate the relationship.

ACCOUNTING FOR STRESS

It is useful to remember that creating a trusting and committed relationship—one based on disclosure and intimacy—can be costly. Moving from a discussion based on orientation dialog, for example, requires a financial planner to sometimes challenge, prompt, or confront a client. Doing so can cause the client to feel stress. Client responses can likewise cause the financial planner to feel stress. It is naive to believe that clients will accept confrontation without pushing back or at times oppose a new viewpoint or suggestion. Added to this mix are nonverbal signs, as described in Chapter 1, which are constantly being received and interpreted.

Recent research in the fields of financial therapy and psychophysiological economics suggests that when clients feel stressed, they are less likely to listen attentively to a financial planner. Additionally, a client's willingness to implement planning recommendations declines if stress becomes unacceptably high.

Figure 2.2 illustrates a typical client stress reaction during a common orientation discussion between a financial planner and prospective client. The graph represents a client's physiological stress, as measured by sweat or skin conductance (as people get stressed they tend to sweat more), of a client recorded in real time. The vertical lines in the graph represent points in the discussion when the financial planner asked the client questions. At the outset of the discussion the questions orientation focused (somewhat superficial and not at all intimate). As the brief discussion unfolded, the financial planner began to ask questions that were marginally more challenging. Questions related to how much the prospect earned, what three financial goals he or she had at the time, and what his or her hopes and dreams were all resulted in increased client stress. As the client's stress increased the client became more anxious about the interview, the situation, and the financial planner. Rather than leading to a relationship built on trust and understanding, the manner in which questions were asked in this scenario caused this particular prospective client to disengage from the planning process. As shown in Figure 2.2, the significant change in stress occurred within a nine-minute period!

Of course, financial planners need to ask questions related to income, net worth, family life, goals, and dreams. The issue is not whether these questions should be asked, but rather when and how these types of queries should be made. Later in this book we will share some particularly powerful communication tools that can be used, even at the orientation phase of a relationship, to effectively reduce stress and promote client confidence. For example, doing something as simple as rearranging the way the financial planner and client are seated when talking can sometimes be enough to reduce client stress enough to promote deeper and more meaningful dialog.

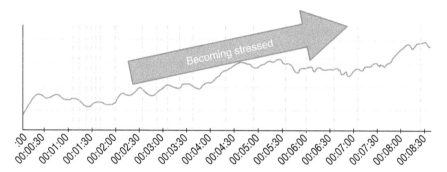

FIGURE 2.2   Client Stress as a Function of Communication Penetration by a Financial Planner

BUILDING CLIENT TRUST: AN APPRECIATIVE INQUIRY EXAMPLE

Ultimately, the choice to continue a client–financial planner relationship is based on an evaluation of how satisfied each participant is in the interpersonal communication process. This evaluation is relatively subjective and taken by both financial planner and client. At the core of this assessment is how well the financial planner and client are communicating—sending, receiving, interpreting (decoding), and resending (encoding) messages. It is on this point that the remainder of this book revolves.

To move through the stages of a relationship—to penetrate interpersonal communication barriers—a financial planner must take control of the communication process. This must occur from the initial moment of orientation exchange. This has less to do with manipulation or direct control over a client and much more to do with ensuring that the ratio of relationship benefits to costs perceived by a client is high. Remember, if a client perceives the benefits of the client–financial planner relationship exceed his or her costs, the client will be much more likely to move through the relationship stages. Because financial planner communication, both verbal and nonverbal, is the primary way in which a client can evaluate benefits and costs, it is imperative that financial planners develop, practice, and continually update their interpersonal communication skills.

VIDEO CLIP 2A

Appreciative Financial Planning Examples

How does asking a question from an AFP perspective differ from a traditional problem-oriented approach? Although this book contains another chapter devoted to the process of developing client trust and commitment through the application of interpersonal communication tools and techniques, the topic is important enough to begin thinking about now. Doney, Cannon, and Mullen[5] defined *trust* as a person's willingness to rely on someone else and to engage in behavior when that action makes them vulnerable to the other person. This is, in a nutshell, the foundation of strong client–financial planner relationships. Clients must form a strong *working alliance* with their financial planner, which is based on trusting that the planner is working in the client's best interest, before they will be willing to implement financial planner–provided recommendations. The level of agreement in the tasks and goals of the overall financial planning process and the emotional bond between the client and the financial planner determines the strength of the client–financial planner working alliance.

In some ways, the pursuit of creating closer, more meaningful bonds with clients is something all financial planning professionals strive to accomplish. Consider the work of Edward Jacobson.[6] He has advocated the adoption of a model he termed "Appreciative Financial Planning" (AFP). AFP is an extension of appreciative inquiry as developed by Cooperrider and Whitney.[7] As an approach to applying the financial planning process, AFP moves client–financial planner discussions away from analyzing past mistakes, losses, and disappointments. Rather than focus on negative outcomes, those who follow an appreciative inquiry approach to communication and planning instead emphasize what a client has done well and what has worked in the past. Here is an example of asking a past, problem-oriented question in which a client lost money:

> "What prompted you to purchase that investment?"
> Someone using an AFP method might instead ask:

> "Tell me something positive that came out of that investment?"

Four elements make up the core of AFP. First, Jacobson encourages financial planners to spend time discovering as much about their client as possible. Second, clients are encouraged to create visions of their financial future that are not bound by past failures or present constraints. The third element involves financial planning activities that are designed to help reach goal achievement. Finally, a plan is delivered. As envisioned by Jacobson, plan delivery is really about becoming a client's most trusted adviser by cementing a strong working alliance. In other words, the financial planner moves from being a technician to being a coach in the eyes of the client.

Appreciative inquiry and AFP are grounded in communication and counseling theory that is quite similar to what has been presented in this chapter as orientation and exploration. There is a common bond among nearly all financial planning approaches that share a goal of creating trust among clients, namely, a shift away from problem solving to affective and stable exchanges.

Conceptually, this transformation in approach is quite simple. In practice, it is very difficult to achieve. Pullen[8] noted that traditional models of financial planning follow a four-step method: (1) identifying a problem, (2) analyzing the problem causes, (3) analyzing and developing problem solutions, and (4) creating an action plan. Pullen argued that this traditional approach fails to create a strong working alliance between a client and financial planner because it directs a client's attention toward negative events, behaviors, and attitudes. The focus is totally on solving problems. While it is often necessary to identify or uncover client financial problems and concerns, an overemphasis on negative issues can be quite depressing and, honestly, a factor that leads people into a state of hopelessness and avoidance. It should be obvious that clients who are focused too heavily on past mistakes, worries about the future, and problems—all of which cause financial stress—will be less likely to fully engage in the process of financial planning. The communication tools and techniques presented in this book, as well as skills advocated within AFP and other models (for example, solution-focused financial planning), are designed to help readers move away from a strict problem-solving approach to one based on trust developed through culturally appropriate orientation, exploration, affective exchange focused on client strengths, and ongoing stable client–financial planner exchanges.

SUMMARY

The process of interpersonal communication often seems to occur naturally. Some people imagine that great communicators are born that way and that great communication between a financial planner and a client is either present or not present. This chapter takes the position that interpersonal communication is, in fact, a learned process. Furthermore, great communication that leads to strong working alliances can be learned, practiced, and improved. The remainder of this book discusses specific ways in which communication theory, as outlined in the opening chapters of this book, can be applied in practice. As noted here, financial planners can gain the trust and commitment of clients only when clients perceive the content, context, and effect of a relationship as being more valuable than the costs associated with what is said or done. For better or worse, the only mechanism available to clients, at the initial stages of a client–financial planner relationship, to best gauge the costs and benefits of a relationship involves interpreting messages sent by the financial planner. When interpersonal communication is viewed as a key element in shaping the perception of costs and benefits, it should be obvious that the most skilled communicators will generally have an advantage over others in creating long-lasting, meaningful, and trusting client–financial planner relationships.

CHAPTER APPLICATIONS

1. Which of the following is not a stage of relationship communication as outlined in social penetration theory?
   a. Orientation
   b. Exploration
   c. Disclosure
   d. Stability

2. From a financial planner's perspective, when the costs associated with maintaining a client–financial planner relationship exceed the benefits received, the planner should
   a. Work harder to move the communication process to a higher stage of dialog
   b. Terminate the relationship
   c. Bring in an outside consultant to reduce client–financial planner conflict
   d. Ask the client additional orientation questions

3. Financial planners who are most likely to develop long-lasting client–financial planner relationships built on trust, intimacy, and disclosure are at what stage of social penetration theory communication?
   a. Orientation
   b. Exploration
   c. Disclosure
   d. Stability

4. Cost forecasting refers to
   a. Projecting planning revenues from a client's outward appearance
   b. Projecting how a client will act in the future based on current behavior
   c. Predicting how long it will take to move from one stage of communication to another
   d. All of the above

5. Stress tends to
   a. Reduce a client's focus and listening skills
   b. Reduce a client's willingness to implement recommendations
   c. Reduce a client's willingness to engage in the planning process
   d. All of the above

6. Mitch tells his client, "I really value your insights." This is an example of a(n):
   a. Affective exchange
   b. Stable exchange
   c. Exploratory exchange
   d. Cost-laden exchange

7. Jacque will most likely terminate the ongoing relationship with her financial planner if:
   a. Relationship Rewards > Relationship Costs
   b. Relationship Costs > Relationship Rewards
   c. Relationship Costs < Relationship Rewards
   d. Relationship Rewards – Relationship Costs = 0

8. Taking control of the communication process is recommended as a way to help a financial planner
   a. Manipulate a client to purchase products
   b. Direct a client to turn over control of financial decision-making to the financial planner
   c. Ensure that the ratio of planning costs to benefits remains high
   d. Enhance the trust a client feels toward her financial planner

9. All of the following are elements of Appreciative Financial Planning except:
   a. Taking time to learn about a client
   b. Encouraging clients to visualize their financial future
   c. Delving into a client's past mistakes and failures
   d. Delivering a financial plan

10. Before client trust can be fully established, a financial planner must:
    a. Reinforce the notion that she is working in the client's best interest
    b. Document that she has consistently outperformed the markets or relevant index
    c. Communicate that she has developed an interpersonal process focused on a manipulative alliance
    d. All of the above

11. Match the following questions and comments to the appropriate stage of communication (orientation, exploration, affective, stable)[10]:
    a. "I enjoy our meetings very much"
    b. "What are your office hours?"
    c. "What do you think of the new tax code?"
    d. "When are you going to do the right thing and marry that woman?"
    e. "Tom, this is my para-planner Pat"
    f. "I am deeply in debt"

12. Read each of the following questions and statements. Determine whether the item is problematically or appreciatively focused[11]:
    a. Tell me what you most enjoy about working for company X?
    b. What is holding you back from retiring this year?
    c. If you were to retire tomorrow, what would a dream year in retirement look like?
    d. Why do you think your spouse spent so much money over the holidays?
    e. What expenses can you cut over the next 30 days?

13. Please provide two examples of statements a financial planner might make for each of the linear stages of client–financial planner communication (that is, orientation, exploration, affective exchanges, and stable exchanges).

14. Regarding the cost/benefit tradeoff, describe three situations in which a client might view the relationship rewards as less than the relationship costs, thus terminating the relationship. Beyond the one example provided in the chapter, what are two other reasons a planner might end a client relationship as explained by cost forecasting?

15. Explain why you agree or disagree with the Appreciative Financial Planning approach. Ask a friend or another student in the class to tell you about a problem he or she is having or a past mistake he or she has made. Try approaching the conversation using appreciative inquiry and describe this experience.

NOTES

1. R. L. Heath and J. Bryant, *Human Communication Theory and Research: Concepts, Contexts, and Challenges* (Hillsdale, NJ: Lawrence Erlbaum Associates, 1992).

2. I. Altman and D. A. Taylor, *Social Penetration: The Development of Interpersonal Relationships* (New York: Holt, Rinehart & Winston, 1973).

3. D. A. Taylor and I. Altman, I "Communication in Interpersonal Relationships: Social Penetration Processes," in *Interpersonal Processes: New Directions in Communication Research*, ed. M. E. Roloff and G. R. Miller (Newbury Park, CA: Sage), 257–277.

4. Readers who are familiar with behavioral theories will find social penetration theory to be similar to social exchange theory (SET). SET argues that people negotiate in ways that reduce costs and increase benefits. Within a financial planning context, SET predicts that client–financial planner relationships will terminate when the room to negotiate higher benefits is exceeded by the costs of obtaining those benefits.

5. P. M. Doney, J. P. Cannon, and M. R. Mullen, "Understanding the Influence of National Culture on the Development of Trust," *Academy of Management Review* 23 (1998): 601–620.

6. E. A. Jacobson, "Appreciative Financial Planning: Harnessing the Power of Appreciative Inquiry for Your Advisory Practice." *Investments and Wealth Monitor* (2009, November/December): 37–45.

7. D. L. Cooperrider and D. Whitney, *Appreciative Inquiry: A Positive Revolution in Change* (San Francisco: Berrett-Koehler Publishers, 2005).

8. C. Pullen, "Money and Soul: Appreciative Inquiry in Financial Planning and Life," *Journal of Financial Planning* 14, no. 10 (2001): 52–54.

CHAPTER 3

Structuring the Process of Communication through the Office Environment

INTRODUCTION

The benefits associated with developing and improving your interpersonal communication skills can be quite impactful. Possibly the most important outcome for financial planners has to do with increased client trust and commitment.[1] Communication, both verbal and nonverbal, is believed to be the most important factor in shaping a client's perceptions of planner competency.[2] While it is true that the technical proficiency, physical appearance, and reputation of a financial planner all play an important role in shaping a client's perceptions, it is the ability to communicate effectively that leads to long-lasting client–financial planner relationships. This insight is a two-edged sword. As noted throughout this book, financial planners who are skilled at listening, framing a client's goals and needs, interpreting client cues, and responding in ways that are supportive and directive have more opportunities to gain the trust of their clients. The downside to this insight is that some advisers may be tempted to use their communication skills and abilities for nefarious purposes. That is, certain financial advisers may find that they can more easily manipulate the attitudes and behaviors of clients through the application of interpersonal communication techniques.

The point of this book is *not* about *client manipulation*. When we talk about manipulation, we mean using the skills you will learn and practice to influence clients in a way that is abusive, deceptive, or misleading. The tools and techniques presented in this book are *not* intended to help a financial adviser close a sale or increase an adviser's prospective client close rate. Certainly, these may be outcomes associated with becoming more proficient interpersonally, but these are secondary side effects. It is our hope that the tools, techniques, and strategies illustrated in this book will be used only in ways that benefit clients in reaching their life dreams and financial goals on the way to enhanced financial well-being. Stated another way, the financial planning communication techniques that are highlighted from this point forward are presented as a way to help financial planners reach out more effectively to a broader spectrum of clientele in ways that improve the lives of clients.

IDENTIFYING TARGET CLIENTELE

A key question that every financial planner needs to answer is: What are the contact preferences and expectations of your target clientele? We believe clients fall into one of two categories that can be framed along a reversing continuum. This can be seen in Figure 3.1. On the left side of the continuum are clients who view the financial planning process as a commodity. That is, these clients view financial planners similarly to real estate agents, tax preparers, plumbers, electricians, and auto mechanics. Clients who fall on the extreme left side of the transaction arrow are willing to work with any adviser who meets the clients' current needs for a product or service. These clients tend to be *transaction oriented*. Other clients may hold less extreme attitudes. They still view the financial planning process as a commodity, but they also may have a desire to find an adviser they can work with on a regular basis. Now, if the adviser is unable to meet a client's needs, the client will likely seek help from someone else. The client will do this without hesitation because he or she does not view the client–financial planner relationship as anything more than a business transaction. Financial planners who target clients in the transactional sphere of the marketplace will have a radically different approach to client communication from financial planners who work with clients seeking *relational partnerships.*

On the other side of the continuum are clients who embrace the notion that financial planning is relational and thus a process. These clients also are interested, primarily, in working with financial advisers whom they will

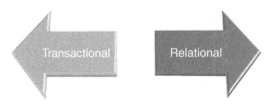

FIGURE 3.1   Continuum of Clientele

trust. For those who are *relationally oriented,* the client–financial planner relationship itself, more so than products, services, or performance, determines whether or not they continue to work with a given particular financial planner.

As was the case with transactional consumers, relational clients fall along a continuum. Those at the far right of the arrow may view their financial adviser as a "therapist," "counselor," "coach," "mentor," or "life adviser." In some ways, these clients will have likely intertwined their personal and professional lives with that of their financial planner. They may not make any significant life choices without consulting their financial planner. This is akin to making the financial planner the clients' most trusted adviser. For many financial planners, this is the dream situation, especially if a small but wealthy clientele can be assembled to support a practice. Other consumers are also driven by the desire to work with someone they can entrust their deepest financial secrets, but they may be somewhat skeptical that a financial planner can fill a broader need. These clients would still be classified as relational clientele, but their commitment to the process may take longer to develop.

It is very important that each financial planner determine if his or her professional home is in the transactional marketplace, and what percentage of clients fall into the transactional category. One way to estimate a percentage answer is to think about how many current clients share the following characteristics by:

- Seeking topic specific advice rather than comprehensive help
- Preferring short meetings
- Accepting the idea of meeting once every couple of years
- Preferring small talk to discussions about goals and dreams
- Rarely talking about legacy issues
- Occasionally or frequently canceling meetings
- Conducting their own research and asking for information to support their findings
- Being reluctant to make referrals
- Being willing to purchase products but hesitant to engage in comprehensive financial planning

The more likely a financial planner is to say, "Yes" that his or her clients match these characteristics, the more likely it is that those clients are transactionally oriented.

Categorizing consumers of financial planning services into two segments originated with research conducted at the University of Georgia and Kansas State University.[3] The research that emerged from clinical studies found two interesting things: first, financial planners, regardless of their primary market, can better improve client outcomes by incorporating basic communication techniques and strategies into their practice. Second, and more important over the long run, financial planners who structure their practice along relational lines generate better performance while maximizing personal wellness. In other words, financial planners who work with relational clients tend to be wealthier and happier.

Although it was already stated earlier in the chapter, it is worth reviewing again. The path to building a practice based on trusting and committed relationships, rather than transactions, is built on the foundation of communication skills. In the rush to learn or refine these skills, it is sometimes easy to overlook the framework of interpersonal communication. Consider a typical solo or small office financial planning practice. The art of communication begins long before a client walks into the office environment. Aspects of marketing, such as an Internet presence, brochures, sponsorships, and other written and broadcast media, all provide a frame of reference for clients. These marketing materials speak to clients in both objective and subjective ways. For example, one firm's marketing materials may conjure images of deep-rooted experience and prestige, while another firm's materials may indicate a more casual planning approach. Prospective clients may have heard from current clients about a financial planner or firm before even making an appointment. These are just the beginning aspects of creating a compelling communication approach. It turns out that the environment in which you have meaningful interactions with clients also matter.

UNDERSTANDING THE OFFICE ENVIRONMENT

Let's jump ahead and assume a client, either through research or referral, makes an appointment to meet with a financial planner. On the day of the appointment, the client will gather requested materials and drive to the financial planner's office. The interpersonal communication process begins when the client parks his or her car and enters the building. We call this the *office environment*. Although few financial planners consider their office environment beyond aesthetic issues, research indicates that clients begin to make judgments about the planning experience primarily through what he or she experiences in the environment. This can be a good thing. It can also be bad.

Imagine the typical office space. The client opens the door and is faced by a receptionist sitting behind a desk or nook. What else does the client experience in that moment? The answer may not be apparent to either the financial planner or the client. Factors such as color, smell, noise, and media all work to form an image of the financial planner's style and competence. Let's look at how these types of factors can influence typical clients.

What is the color of the carpet? What color are the walls painted? Are there pictures, and if yes, what are the themes? Does the furniture fit the size and color of the room? Is there a waiting room, and if yes, are clients encouraged to watch television? Answers to these questions determine, in part, how a client will feel about the planning experience. These feelings are almost always developed before meeting with a financial planner. Think of it this way: the planning process may be harmed if office environment elements are not fully considered and designed. Financial planners often hire interior designers to create amazing spaces, only to find that the space itself conveys an unhelpful impression to clients. For example, having a receptionist sit behind a large fully enclosed desk or cubicle may provide an excellent work space, but this seating and welcoming arrangement also communicates to clients that the planning experience may be transactional. Why? Because a desk represents a barrier between the client and the planning staff. This establishes a hierarchical order of authority. Think about an old-fashioned bank. Not only is there a wall between customers and staff, there might even be bars! Having a desk stand between a client and the planning staff may be perfect if, in fact, a financial planner's practice is transactional. If a financial planner is attempting to build a practice based on relational aspects, however, this simple design choice can be detrimental to meeting that goal.

How is it possible, some might ask, that the choice of desk or table could communicate the planning style of the adviser so clearly? Basically, clients process information quickly based on experience, norms, and expectations. These mental processes create *physiological changes* in the body. Specifically, stress levels can be increased or decreased based on a client's reactions to the office environment. A problem arises when clients experience stress. Nearly all of the research conducted on the associations between psychological processes and physiological outcomes suggest that as stress passes a critical point, the likelihood of a client engaging in comprehensive planning diminishes. Too much stress, in other words, is detrimental to the client–financial planner relationship.[4] In the example just described, the fully enclosed desk will most often be perceived as a barrier to entry. That is, most clients view someone sitting behind a desk as the person who is in place to limit access to the facility. Few financial planners see the role of their receptionist in this way. Most would say that they want the first person of contact—the receptionist—to be friendly, warm, engaging, and only a gatekeeper in regard to scheduling and minimizing unwanted business solicitations. Few use a receptionist as a guard.[5] Yet, the act of placing a barrier between a client and planning staff is generally perceived as exactly the opposite of the planner's intentions. Unfortunately, from the moment the client walks into the office, his or her stress level is already increasing.

Rarely does a client walk through a reception area directly into a financial planner's office. Most often, the client is directed to a waiting area. Think about a typical waiting room, lounge, or office space. Some firms have clients sit in front of or to the side of the receptionist. This is similar to waiting in a medical office. Not much fun, and in some ways, very stressful. Other firms have a dedicated space for their clients to relax before a meeting. Let's envision one such space. The room is probably near the front of the building. Five or six chairs, typically minimalistic office chairs, are aligned along the walls. In the corner is a large flat screen television. Depending on the office policy, or the whims of the receptionist, a business news program may be turned on. This is logical. A financial planner might conclude the clients should know what is happening in the financial markets before the meeting.

Is this assumption correct? In reality, visual media, such a television, can be perceived as a stressor by some clients.[6] *Stressors* are what lead to increased levels of stress. Remember, elevated levels of stress often lead to negative reactions among clients. The existing research indicates that clients watch financial news in general, but bullish investment (positive) news in particular, tend to become highly arousing to them. Watching positive financial news, more so than negative broadcasts, is related to feelings of regret. That is, clients mentally kick themselves for not being invested when the markets are surging forward. This causes stress. On the other hand, when market performance, as reported through the media, is bearish, clients often dismiss the news as being out of their control. Although negative news is also a stressor, its effect is less pronounced.

Does this mean that financial planners should sit their clients in a waiting room and broadcast negative financial news? The answer is clearly no. What the research indicates is that clients should not be exposed to any type of media—be it television or radio—before a client–financial planner meeting that has not been thoroughly screened for content. For example, showing a home improvement show in which the show's stars are experiencing financial losses can just as easily create stress among clients as a market update on a business news channel. Financial planners who turn on a television without thinking are inadvertently introducing a stressor into their office environment. This should be avoided.[7]

This last point is of critical importance in terms of facilitating effective interpersonal communication. Financial planners who are interested in developing practices based on relational elements must take steps to manage how clients experience and interpret the planning process. This begins, as the examples from earlier in this chapter highlight, the moment a client

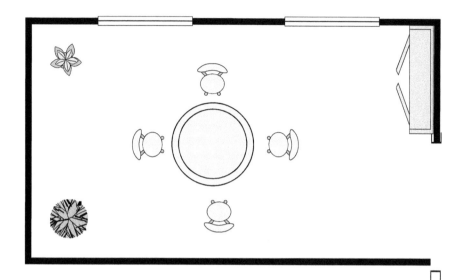

FIGURE 3.2   Traditional Seating Arrangement That Induces Client Stress

enters the office environment. If clients are at ease, comfortable, and in a low state of stress, they will be more likely to engage in meaningful conversation, more prone to disclose personal, family, and financial information, and most importantly, more inclined to implement financial planning recommendations.[8] As dialog continues over time, in a low stress environment, the client will increasingly look to their financial planner as a trusted adviser. This trust will be built on shared values, commitment, and confidence.

Let's now look at the number one source of environmental stress within the planning process: the *office seating arrangement*.[9] Imagine the client is now sitting in the financial planner's office. Figure 3.2 represents a typical financial planning office space. Is this setup a stress inducer or reducer? In general, clients experience any situation in which a *barrier* exists between the client and financial planner as a stressor. In Figure 3.2, the table itself can be framed as a communication barrier. As such, financial planners who regularly meet with clients using this type of arrangement can expect their clients to be more stressed than those who meet with planners using some other seating arrangement.

Is the situation significantly different, for better or worse, if a financial planner meets with clients in a *conference room* setting? Figure 3.3 illustrates a typical conference room arrangement. In the figure, a flat-screen monitor sits on one end of the table. The financial planner sits at the head of the table, and the clients—assuming a couple, in this example—might sit

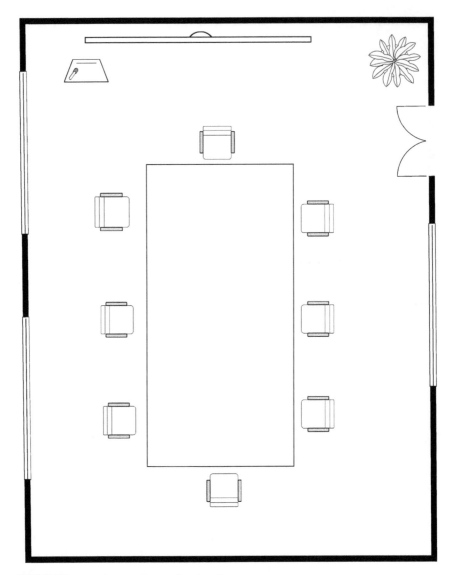

FIGURE 3.3   Conference Room Seating Arrangement

together across from the financial planner. Unfortunately, this meeting setup is no better as a stress reducer than meeting around a table. In fact, this situation may induce increased stress on the part of all parties, especially if the couple is seated across from each other. Increased stress occurs because now the client partners have created a barrier between themselves, which may

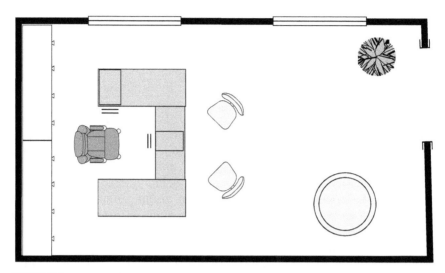

FIGURE 3.4 Financial Planner's Office Designed for Transactional Planning

act as a hindrance to open dialog, full disclosure, and sharing. The financial planner in this situation is also shut off from both clients. If the clients sit next to each other, the person farthest away from the financial planner may feel disengaged, underappreciated, and unheard. None of these states of mind are conducive to building strong client–financial planner relationships.

One more example serves to illustrate the point that the office environment can act as an important tool or roadblock in the communication process. Consider Figure 3.4. This meeting arrangement is very typical in the financial planning profession. Nearly all entry-level and some experienced financial planners meet clients in an office. In one section of the office is the door and maybe a filing cabinet or credenza. A desk and bookcase make up the remainder of the office. In front of the desk sit two office chairs—not particularly comfortable, but functional. When meeting with clients, the financial planner sits behind the desk, sometimes in a leather office chair that both swivels and moves up and down. The client(s) sits in front of the desk, often looking up at the financial planner whose chair is elevated. What does this do to the communication dynamic in the room? Unfortunately, this arrangement can generate elevated levels of client stress. The seating arrangement nonverbally communicates that the financial planning process is transactional, not at all relational. Using this approach to conduct client interviews is totally appropriate when buying a car, having taxes completed, or visiting with an attorney, but the setup is counterproductive in regard to establishing trusting client–financial planner relationships.

Client meeting spaces, like those shown in Figures 3.2, 3.3, and 3.4, are not beneficial to promoting relational interpersonal communication. Some may argue that even so, it is impossible to conduct meaningful financial planning engagements without a desk or table of some sort. Is this true? Of course, this argument is true some of the time, but certainly less often than might be expected. Consider an initial client–financial planner meeting. What is the purpose of an initial meeting? Is it to sell a product? If yes, then using a table to display product information and to facilitate the signing of forms is important.[10] If the answer is to learn more about the client, to better understand their goals and dreams, and to better grasp why they want to engage in the planning process, the need for a table or other barrier is relatively valueless. What is important is providing an environment that helps frame a financial planner not as a transaction-based adviser but rather as someone who can be trusted with deep and meaningful information.

How does a financial planner design such an environment? The answer may appear to be riddled with risk. At least this is true if someone attempts to answer the question with previous notions of what a financial planner's office environment is supposed to look like. Traditionally, for example, it was assumed that financial planners should design their office spaces to resemble a country-home den, country club dining room, or an office in an upscale private bank. That is, financial planners were encouraged to use many dark colors, a liberal use of leather seating, and a hushed tone muffled by deep plush carpet. The effect, or hoped-for outcome, of such a design scheme was to impress clients with an image of stability and wealth. In other words, the key design element was one focused on communicating the benefits of uniting with the firm—similar to joining an exclusive country club. There is nothing inherently wrong with presenting this image. The only difficulty is that the notion of creating barriers between clients and planners is implied in the design. It was once thought that the financial planner needed to set himself or herself apart from the client and appear as a financial expert rather than a trusted adviser. The good news is that for those financial planners who work primarily with transactional clients, this office setup can be quite effective. The problem is that it may communicate the wrong message for clients who are seeking a different type of client–financial planner relationship.

Assuming that a financial planner's primary communication goal is to promote deep, long-lasting, and trusting relationships with clients, the initial meeting, and all subsequent meetings where client note taking and signatures are not needed, generally should take place in barrier-free rooms. Figure 3.5 shows what a simple *financial therapy office* might look like. Two key elements are in place in the room. First, a comfortable couch or oversized chair for the client. Second, a similar colored or upholstered chair

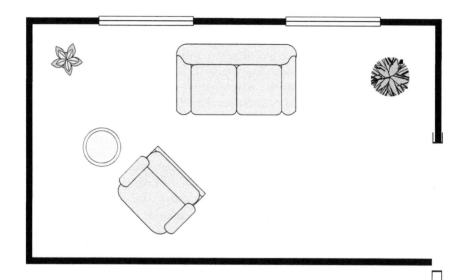

FIGURE 3.5 Financial Therapy Seating Arrangement

for the financial planner. Notice too that the room is relatively clean, with maybe a live plant or two and just a few simple pictures. A small table is available and close to the financial planner's chair. As shown, the table is functional but not a barrier. Notice as well how the couch and chair are situated. The general rule is to situate the furniture between 90- and 150-degree angles to each other.[11] The financial planner's chair should be arranged so that any windows are behind the client.[12] It is important for any clocks in the room be placed so that only the financial planner can see the time.[13] When describing the effectiveness of this therapeutic seating arrangement, Benjamin[14] stated the following:

"This arrangement works best for me. The interviewee can face me when he wishes to do so, and at other times he can look straight ahead without my getting in his way. I am equally unhampered" (p. 3).

It is not uncommon for financial planners to object to this type of client meeting room on two grounds. The first deals with the lack of a table upon which to show forms, documents, and marketing materials. The second is the corresponding need for a writing surface upon which to take notes. These objections, of course, must be framed with the practice management approach used by the financial planner. These are completely valid arguments if it is assumed that only the financial planner can take notes, the financial planner should take notes, and clients prefer hard copy forms and marketing materials. Much of the research on client communication indicates that none of these working assumptions is universally correct. Let's look at each.

Therapists, counselors, psychologists, and other mental health professionals have long known and acknowledged that many clients are offended by constant note taking on the part of their adviser. Rarely does taking notes enhance interpersonal communication. The reason for this is simple. Taking notes diverts the note taker's attention away from the client and what the client is saying. Both verbal and nonverbal client cues can easily be missed in the midst of note taking. Assuming that a financial planner must take notes during a meeting, it is not only possible but easily accomplished using a clipboard or a tablet. Typically, the financial planner will sit, relaxed, and with legs crossed in his or her chair. The clipboard or tablet can rest comfortably on the lap as notes are entered. This approach allows for eye contact between client and planner. If notes are going to be taken, the financial planner should introduce this fact at the outset of the meeting. Additional communication strategies will be provided in later chapters for financial planners who are still nervous about the thought of engaging clients in conversation without taking notes.

VIDEO 3A

Taking Notes While Seated

How does this financial planner manage to listen to the client while taking effective notes?

The paradoxical question is why a financial planner needs to take notes. It is quite common in today's modern practices for a *para-planner* to be present in initial and some ongoing client meetings. Given rules of confidentiality and privacy laws, few clients object to someone else taking notes during a meeting. There certainly may be situations in which a client wishes to meet solely with the financial planner. In these cases, the financial planner and a staff member can summarize notes after the meeting.

The last objection deals with how forms and marketing materials should be presented to clients in the absence of a table or desk. Although the research is limited, experimental studies in which men and women were asked to respond to hard copy and media-delivered assessments indicates that clients tend to prefer viewing materials on screen rather than on paper.[15] A large, flat screen monitor can easily be incorporated into an office, such as the one shown in Figure 3.3. Using a tablet or other remote prompter, all of a client's forms, relevant disclosures, and other documents can be shown and viewed

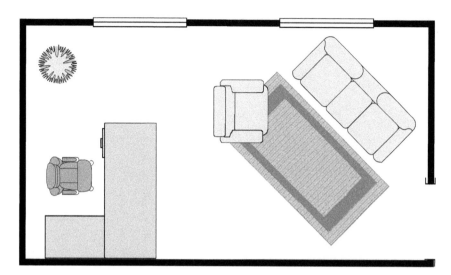

FIGURE 3.6 Redesigned Financial Planner Therapeutic Office Space

on the monitor. Many clients—especially those looking for a relationship rather than a transaction—may prefer this method of discussion.[16]

For many financial planners, the office arrangement shown in Figure 3.5 may be too extreme for their practice. Others may find that they are too space-constrained to create a separate meeting area consisting solely of this type of furniture. Fortunately, financial planners can adapt aspects of the therapeutic model into almost any existing office space. Consider Figure 3.6. This graphic shows how a typical office can be altered simply by removing office chairs and adding comfortable high-back chairs. Notice too that in Figure 3.6 a small coffee table could easily be added. A coffee table, while still a barrier between a client and the financial planner, is less obtrusive than a standard table, yet effective for use when making presentations and for form signing.

Figure 3.7 illustrates yet another way the therapeutic model can be incorporated into a financial planning office environment. In this design, four comfortable chairs surround a modest coffee table. A large flat screen monitor can be used to view important documents. Note also the inclusion of live plants. Typically, this seating arrangement is best used in offices in which external distractions, such as windows or open doors, are not present.

All of the discussion and tools and techniques described in this chapter have been focused on one primary outcome: to help a financial planner manage the stress felt by a client before and during a client–financial

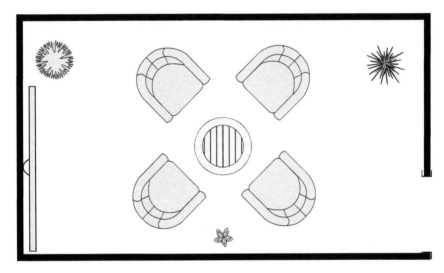

FIGURE 3.7   Alternative Financial Planner Therapeutic Office Space

planner meeting. As highlighted earlier, the office environment provides the first, and often ongoing, expression of a financial planner's practice management approach. Planners who are primarily interested in establishing relationships based on trust and commitment with clients who are looking for a trusted adviser, compared to someone who is primarily interested in transacting business, should seriously consider what their office communicates to clients. In the end, client stress matters. The more stress experienced, the less likely the client will enthusiastically engage in the financial planning process. On the other hand, the more ways a financial planner can reduce client stress within the environment, the more likely he or she is going to be viewed as competent, trustworthy, and caring by clients.

STRESS AND COMMUNICATION: BRINGING THE PIECES TOGETHER

Before moving on to descriptions of specific verbal and nonverbal communication techniques, it is worth taking a moment to review the relationship between stress and communication effectiveness. After reading this chapter, some readers may conclude that any level of client stress exhibited by a client may be detrimental to the client–financial planner relationship. This is, quite candidly, not true. Every prospective and current client must experience some degree of arousal in order to prompt action.

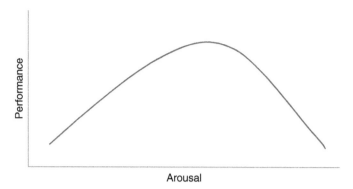

FIGURE 3.8   Relationship Between Arousal and Performance

Think about it from the perspective of a coach and team. An important role of a coach is to ensure that her team is ready to play at peak performance. Look at Figure 3.8. This figure is sometimes called the Yerkes-Dodson model. The vertical axis represents a team member's performance. The horizontal axis is the player's *arousal levels*—a stress reaction. As illustrated, performance and arousal move hand in hand, until arousal becomes too high. When this happens, performance drops. This helps explain why teams play upbeat music during pregame warm-ups and chant together right before a game. It also helps explain why coaches take steps during the game to generate arousal with some players while tamping down enthusiasm for other players.

In the context of financial planning, a financial planner is akin to a coach. A client is, using this example, a player. Unless the client is engaged and aroused by the prospect of taking action, he or she may be too apathetic or disengaged to implement planning recommendations. In other words, it is up to the financial planner to generate some arousal to help move a client toward plan implementation. The problem comes when a client becomes overly aroused or stimulated. Just like an athlete whose performance will drop off, placing a client under too much pressure can result in disengagement and a reduction in trust and commitment.

SUMMARY

One way to think about the office environment as a stressor is to visualize stressors as building on one another. The best types of financial stressors—those that help move a client from inaction to implementation—are those that force clients to think about their goals, dreams, financial situation, and other choice scenarios. A financial planner adds arousal to the client–financial planner relationship by probing meaningful issues with the client. If the process gets out of control, however, the generation of arousal can lead a client to question the foundational aspects of a financial plan. This is the reason it is so crucial to carefully plan out the office environment. There is no reason to preload a client's level of arousal with essentially trivial office environment elements. If left to chance, the moment other financial planning stressors are added to the mix, the client can easily become overwhelmed. As illustrated in this chapter, there really is no need to go down this path. Financial planners who don't leave client stressors to chance—at least those they can control—have a much better chance of being seen a trusted adviser.

CHAPTER APPLICATIONS

1. What are the two ends of a continuum in which financial planning clients can be categorized?
   a. Contented and independent
   b. Transactional and relational
   c. Probing and passive
   d. Therapeutic and directional

2. A client who rarely talks about legacy issues and is reluctant to make referrals likely views the client–financial planner relationship as
   a. Therapeutic
   b. Relational
   c. Directional
   d. Transactional

3. Stressors can cause
   a. Physiological changes in the body
   b. A desire among some clients to terminate the planning relationship
   c. Deeper and improved dialog between client and planner
   d. Both a and b

4. Which of the following is the number one source of environmental stress within the planning process?
   a. The color of a planner's carpeting
   b. Allowing clients to watch television in a waiting room
   c. Forcing clients to sit in the same room as a receptionist
   d. The office seating arrangement

5. Financial planners who want to minimize client stress as a way to forge deeper and committed relationships with clients should meet prospective clients in which type of office space?
   a. In a room with a table large enough to allow the sharing of documents
   b. In a room in which business and finance television programming is being watched

    c. In a room with a comfortable chair and couch

    d. In a room with the planner behind his or her desk and the client sitting in front of the desk

6. A client who is looking to build a relationship with a financial planner will tend to exhibit which of the following characteristics?

    I. Be willing to make referrals

    II. Rarely cancel meetings

    III. Enjoy talking about financial goals and dreams

    a. III only

    b. I and II only

    c. II and III only

    d. I, II, and III

7. Michelle is meeting with a client. She is sitting on one side of an office table directly across from her client. She likes the table because she can spread out paperwork and take notes more efficiently. She has noticed, however, that her clients rarely move beyond the transactional stage of client–financial planner interactions. What is most likely causing this lack of client commitment?

    a. The use of the table may be creating a barrier between Michelle and her clients.

    b. She is not inducing enough stress into the client–financial planning relationship.

    c. She is failing to prompt her clients to take action because the table makes clients think she is a receptionist.

    d. All of the above are true.

8. When building an office space in which clients will have meetings with a financial planner or staff, it is acceptable for the space to include:

    a. Comfortable chairs

    b. A couch or love seat

    c. Plants

    d. All of the above

9. A client's seat should:

    a. Face the office window

    b. Have a clear view of a clock

    c. Both a and b

    d. None of the above

10. Which of the following statements is true in relation to managing a client's stress level?

    a. It is important to eliminate a client's stress within the office environment.

    b. Inducing some degree of stress or arousal will help prompt a client to take action.

    c. Because the relationship between stress and performance is positive, it is important for financial planners to keep a client's arousal level high before making a recommendation.

    d. Stress reduction is important to encourage client implementation, whereas increases in stress should be used as a way to gather client data.

11. Review the list of questions that can be used to classify clients as being transactional. Use this list to categorize your existing client base. Approximately what percentage of clients can be classified as transactional? Finally, do your current clients represent the marketplace in which you want to work?

12. Make a sketch of your current office space (or of a financial planning professional you know). After reviewing how the furniture is laid out in the room, do you think that your office is more or less conducive to transactional or relational planning? How can you redesign your office space to make it more inviting to clients who are looking for a relationship rather than a transaction?

13. Imagine you were in a situation that necessitated the long-term and regular assistance of an attorney. As such, you've set up three consultation meetings with well-respected attorneys in your local community to help you decide whom to hire through an annual retainer. What room setup would you prefer for having an hour-long meeting with each attorney. Why do you prefer this setup?

14. In regard to the time and skills associated with communication, what would you imagine to be some of the costs and benefits of working with clients seeking relational partnerships as compared to working with clients in the transactional sphere of the marketplace?

15. Besides furniture layout and the use of large visual aids, what other office environment factors communicate messages to clients or might affect clients' stress levels (for example, think about how the physical environment influences the traditional five senses of a client)?

NOTES

1. C. Anderson and D. L. Sharpe, "The Efficacy of Life Planning Communication Tasks in Developing Successful Client-Financial Planner Relationships," *Journal of Financial Planning* 21, no. 6 (2008): 66–77.
2. S. Neeru and P. G. Patterson, "The Impact of Communication Effectiveness and Service Quality on Relationship Commitment in Consumer, Professional Services," *Journal of Services Marketing* 13 (1999): 151–170.
3. A. Herbers, "Stress Fracture," *Investment Advisor* 32, no. 11 (2012): 24–35.
4. J. E. Grable and S. L. Britt, "Assessing Client Stress and Why It Matters to Financial Advisors," *Journal of Financial Service Professionals* 3 (2012): 39–46.
5. Isn't this the way most insurance, legal, tax, and service firms welcome their clients? The reason is that nearly all service providers, and generally all product companies, mechanics, for example, view interactions with clients on a transactional basis.
6. J. E. Grable and S. L. Britt, "Financial News and Client Stress: Understanding the Association from a Financial Planning Perspective," *Financial Planning Review* 5, no. 3 (2012): 23–36.
7. An alternative involves developing a looping video or DVD that presents marketing images of the firm, client testimonials, and interesting pictures and

graphics that might appeal to the financial goals and dreams of the planner's target clientele.

8. Stress creates a "fight or flight" response in most humans. As stress increases, a person's first and natural reaction is either to object, argue, or fight what is being presented or to flee or exit the source of the stress. If a financial planner's office environment acts as a stressor, this "fight or flight" response will be present from the outset of the initial discussion, thus creating an extra communication barrier the financial planner must overcome.

9. S. L. Britt and J. E. Grable, "Your Office May Be a Stressor: Understand How the Physical Environment of Your Office Affects Financial Counseling Clients," *The Standard* 30, no. 2 (2012): 5 and 13.

10. Some would argue, nonetheless, that a conversation without barriers will improve the likelihood that the prospective client will buy the product. At the point of sale, the meeting can be moved to a conference room or other place where documents can be signed.

11. J. Sommers-Flanagan and R. Sommers-Flanagan, *Foundations of Therapeutic Interviewing* (Needham Heights, MA: Allyn & Bacon, 1993).

12. This arrangement reduces the possibility that a client will become distracted.

13. Having the clock only in view of the financial planner ensures that the meeting can be conducted in a timely and efficient manner.

14. A. Benjamin, *The Helping Interview*, 3rd ed. (Boston: Houghton-Mifflin, 1981).

15. There are limited exceptions to this general rule. For example, some clients, who are classified at kinesthetic learners—they learn through experience, touching, and feeling—prefer to hold paper as opposed to viewing the same form through a television or computer monitor. At most, one out of five clients can be classified as kinesthetic learners. The remainder tend to be auditory or visual learners.

16. Men tend to respond most favorably to viewing and responding to financial documentation through media.

4

Listening Skills

We sometimes are asked to provide consulting insights to firms wanting to improve their communication effectiveness. Many times our recommendation to members of the firm's planning staff boils down to this:

> Before saying anything, listen to the client. Stop and listen. Listen to the words spoken. Listen to the words unspoken. When you can stand it no more, and you must talk, stop. Listen again. Only then should you talk.

We stress the importance of listening because few people actually practice this skill. Nearly all financial planners, if asked, say they are a good listener. For most financial planners (and people in general), however, this is not true. Being a good listener requires a substantial amount of conscious effort and practice. Although often not very effectively, listening is something we all do to some extent in our everyday conversations. This leaves many financial planners taking this particular communication skill for granted.

As it turns out, people often think they are listening when in fact they are really constructing a thought or response based on their own opinion or need to be heard. They should, however, be focused on what the other person is saying. This is where the effort to stay engaged with the other person and to practice "listening" comes into play. If you are an aspiring financial planner, our recommendation is to practice listening in all aspects of your life. Practice will help you become a good listener, and ultimately a much better financial planner, when you enter the profession and face clients face to face. If you are already a financial planner, our recommendation happens to be the same: practice listening. You can do this right now. Listen to what your colleagues are saying. Don't interrupt them or anticipate their next word or sentence. Sit back and enjoy the process. Do the same thing with your clients. You might learn some interesting things. Even the most experienced practitioner can reflect upon her listening skills and discover ways to improve. With the appropriate amount of knowledge and practice, the communication skill of listening will continue to develop and evolve and eventually require less conscious effort.

Financial planners commonly emphasize their surprise at how exhausted they feel after meeting with a client for an initial consultation when they are focused on being a good listener. When a financial planner transforms from a good listener to someone with a mastery of listening, they are better able to concentrate on the client and interpret what is being said. Rather than focusing on constructing a response when listening, this financial planner is focusing on what is being said, what it means, and why it is being said. As will be illustrated throughout this chapter, listening may be the single most powerful communication tool for those financial planners who want to build a strong working alliance with clients. The listening process has three components[1]: (1) attention to the client, (2) attention to what is heard, and (3) interpreting what is heard. This chapter addresses each of these elements. Regardless of how many years a financial planner may have in meeting with clients on a face-to-face basis, reviewing and practicing these elements of listening can improve outcomes when working with clients.

PAYING ATTENTION TO THE CLIENT

The first element of effective listening involves paying attention to the client. Some may assume this is an obvious and easy task, but in fact, maintaining attention can be quite difficult. As with nearly every other aspect of interpersonal communication, the ability to focus attention on another person is a learned skill. Ivey and Gluckerstern (1984)[2] called attention proficiencies listening *microskills*. Their list of microskills includes:

- Being able to face a client in a relaxed and attentive manner
- Using appropriate posture, including being open to the client
- Maintaining ongoing and consistent eye contact
- Effectively using body language, including leaning forward as a way to convey closeness during client discussions
- Maintaining an open mind while delaying immediate judgments
- Being tolerant of client ambiguity, especially during prospective client meetings

Each of these listening microskills helps build rapport with a client. Three microskills are of particular importance: (1) making eye contact,

(2) using appropriate body language, and (3) employing voice mannerisms effectively. Many communication experts consider the task of making and holding *eye contact* to be of singular importance when a person is engaged in interpersonal communication. There is no set rule as to what is appropriate regarding the duration someone should hold the gaze of another person, but there are benchmarks.

- Attempting to hold eye contact with someone for more than approximately 70 percent of the time becomes distracting, intimidating, and counterproductive.
- When not making direct eye contact, it is appropriate to focus, either directly or subtly, on the client's forehead, mouth, or face when he or she is talking.
- When speaking, it is not as necessary to maintain eye contact.

Ivey (1988)[3] provided an interesting tip for those who want to master the art of eye contact. Ivey found that a client's eyes will dilate when they, during a conversation, are engaged. On the other hand, pupils will constrict when the client is bored, disengaged, or distracted. By evaluating this simple indicator, a financial planner can better gauge a client's interest in the conversation.

VIDEO 4A

Video Clip 4A demonstrates body language that generally promotes positive client reactions.

While watching the video, see if you can identify the following:

1. Three examples of body language that are positive
2. At least one example of body language that can result in a negative client reaction

---

The appropriate use of *body language* as a listening microskill is an important theme throughout this book. Ivey (1988)[4] termed body language as both kinesics and proxemics. *Kinesics* refers to factors related to the physical movement of the body or body parts. *Proxemics* denotes the space or other environmental variables—for example, the distance two people sit apart—that frame a conversation.[5] Table 1 highlights some of the most important body language factors categorized by either positive or negative outcomes.

As this list highlights, good listening skills include more than focusing on a client and intently listening to the other person. Clients need to know

TABLE 4.1 Body Language Outcomes

Behavior That Prompts Positive Client Reaction	Behavior That Prompts Negative Client Reaction
Sitting in a relaxed manner	Sitting rigid and stiff
Leaning toward the client	Leaning away from the client
Keeping arms, hands, legs, and feet open to the client	Folding arms and legs in front of client
Sitting about one to two arm's lengths away from client	Sitting closer than one arm's length from client or sitting too far away from client
Eliminating barriers between planner and client	Placing furniture or other barrier between planner and client
Matching a client's facial expressions	Making strange or confusing facial expressions

that they are being heard. A financial planner's body language is a tool that can be used to say, "I am listening and following your words." On the other hand, the wrong body language, intentionally or otherwise, can send a negative communication message to clients.

Employing *voice mannerisms* effectively is the third important listening microskill. The human voice is composed of *intensity, pitch, rate,* and *smoothness.*[6] Parents often teach their children about these four speaking elements by stressing that everyone has an "inside" and an "outside" voice. An inside voice is appropriate for discussion inside the home, office, or other physical place, whereas someone's outside voice can be used in places where high volume talking, yelling, laughing, and other discourse is not only allowed but encouraged. Sommers-Flanagan and Sommers-Flanagan (1993, p. 55)[7] made the following astute observation in relation to the elements of voice mannerisms: "Often, interpersonal influence is determined not so much by what you say but how you say it."

Following (or influencing) the client's preferred or natural tempo of a session is referred to as *pacing* and is a powerful technique in building and maintaining the client-planner working alliance. This pacing or leading refers to the amount of direction the financial planner exerts on the client. The manner in which a client speaks should dictate the response mannerism of the financial planner, particularly when in the initial stages of building rapport. For example, if a client speaks softly and in a low tone, the financial planner may do the same as a way of *mirroring* the client, as a form of pacing. As the client's volume or tone increases, the planner should do the same thing, in most situations. There are times, however, when a financial planner should use intensity, pitch, rate, and smoothness to counteract the content of a client's discussion. Generally, low volume, soft tones, a deep-pitched voice, and fluency of sentence structure can produce more profound explorations of moods, thoughts, and opinions on the part of clients. A gentle voice can very often calm an inflated or intense situation. On the other hand, it may sometimes be important to send a message of expertise and competence. This can be accomplished by raising the volume and tone of speech.[8] There are also times when it makes sense for a financial planner to increase the pacing, which can be accomplished by asking leading questions or providing greater direction in the communication.

ATTENDING TO WHAT IS SAID

The second element in the process of listening involves *attending* to what a client says. Attending means learning to hear and confirm what is spoken. There is a difference between perceiving and comprehending what a client says. This is known as *situational awareness.*[9] Consider the following scenario. Assume a client comes in one day and announces that she is going to quit her job. As a financial planner, you may perceive that the client is feeling stressed about elements of her current job. While this insight is important, it will be difficult to design a recommendation or plan of action regarding the client's situation without first obtaining a deeper comprehension of the situation. It may be that the client's statement about quitting is simply an immediate reaction to a colleague's hostile behavior, in which case counseling the client may be what is necessary. On the other hand, the statement may be an indication of extreme uneasiness that requires a more pronounced analysis of the client's alternatives.

VIDEO 4B

Video 4B illustrates ways a financial planner can send the wrong interpersonal communication message to a client. In this clip, see if you can identify the following negative behavior:

1. Becoming distracted
2. Using poor nonverbal communication skills such as crossing legs and arms and leaning away from the client
3. Avoiding eye contact

Sommers-Flanagan and Sommers-Flanagan (1993)[10] referred to listening and attending to a client's *verbal tracking*. Attending to a client's words involves demonstrating that you are, in fact, tracking what is being said in an active and engaged manner.[11] While advanced aspects of verbal tracking—summarizing, paraphrasing, and so on—is discussed in more detail in later chapters, it is important at this juncture of skill development to focus on the core issue of attending. Often, the easiest, and sometimes best, way to confirm that you are listening and tracking a client's communication is to periodically repeat back what has been stated. This is a way to confirm that you are engaged in the interpersonal communication process with a client.

Research on verbal tracking clearly shows that financial planners are best served by minimizing their personal opinions and reactions associated with what a client is discussing, at least initially. Stated another way, it is more important to listen and be quiet than it is to confront or contradict a client during data gathering and strategizing meetings. As the client–financial planner relationship blossoms over time, there will be ample opportunities to share insights, opinions, and reactions—even those that contradict a client's core belief system. Although it is easier said than done, there is one key rule associated with attending behavior, namely, *stay focused on the client*. During this phase of the listening process, every attempt should be made to keep the client's words and actions at the center of your own thoughts. Again, this is sometimes more difficult to do in practice than in theory.

An effective way to better understand verbal tracking and attending is to find counterexamples of optimal communication. Consider the following list of financial planner behaviors, both verbal and nonverbal, which conveys a message that what the client is saying is being discounted[12]:

- Overusing attending behavior, such as constant head nodding
- Regularly uttering, "Uh huh" or "right"
- Diverting eye contact for extended periods of time
- Turning away from a client
- Folding arms across chest when the client is speaking
- Leaning back away from the client when he or she is speaking
- Becoming visibly distracted while the client is talking

INTERPRETING WHAT IS HEARD

The third element in the listening process involves *interpreting* what is heard. Within therapeutic settings, this is sometimes referred to as "listening with a third ear."[13] This implies that clients communicate using two levels of language. Clients speak using surface-level words, mannerisms, and language. Within the context of situational awareness, words help you perceive what a client is saying. Words, mannerisms, and language also tell a story using deeper meanings. This is where comprehension comes into play. Consider a typical client–financial planner discussion:

> Planner: "Have you thought about refinancing your mortgage?"
>
> Client: "Oh sure, but I have heard rates might go lower."
>
> Planner: "That is certainly a possibility, but it is just as likely that mortgage rates could go up in the next few weeks or months."
>
> Client: "Why do you say that?"
>
> Planner: "This morning the Federal Reserve released data on inflation, and the numbers came in much higher than anyone expected."
>
> Client: "I didn't know that, but anyway, isn't refinancing kind of expensive?"
>
> Planner: "It can be, but we can run the numbers to determine what the after-tax cost will be."
>
> Client: "Well, I just don't know. Maybe we should hold off for a bit to see where things settle out."

On the surface, this discussion seems straightforward. The financial planner starts by suggesting the client think about refinancing her mortgage. The client responds negatively to the suggestion. After presenting clear evidence that now may be the best time to take action, the client moves the discussion toward postponement of a decision. Again, this is what has occurred on the surface.

What is the client really saying in this example? What is the deeper meaning? Looking more deeply into the client's words as a way to comprehend the client's feelings, the financial planner might interpret the discussion differently. It is entirely possible that the client is saying something like:

> "I hear what you are saying. This is probably a good time to refinance my mortgage, but I don't know what to do. If I refinance now and rates go down, I will feel regretful of my decision. If I don't refinance, I will feel like an idiot. Either way, I lose, so I might as well do nothing."

VIDEO 4C

Video 4C illustrates how a planner can deal with possible transference from the client that might have an adverse impact on the client–financial planner working alliance unless effectively addressed.

Notice how the financial planner addresses this possibility in a nonconfrontational, inquisitive way. Ask yourself whether the financial planner fully addressed the potential transference and subsequent tear in the working alliance that led to an even stronger emotional bond with the client. A natural response for many planners is to deflect the potential tension by simply changing the subject. Would this strategy have been as effective?

As this example illustrates, words spoken by a client sometimes have two meanings: a surface meaning and a deeper connotation. It is important to note, however, that more often than not, a client means exactly what they say. Clues that a deeper meaning may be in play include times when a client:

- Avoids a direct decision
- Attempts to redirect questions
- Moves questions and answers to a different level

For example, if a client responds with a joke to a serious question, this may indicate that the financial planner's queries are distressful for the client. In response, the client may attempt to disguise his or her true feelings and intentions through the use of distracting surface words.

In the preceding example, a financial planner who is skilled at listening would likely pull back from direct questions about interest rates and refinancing choices. Diverting the discussion to a review of risk and return tradeoffs, behavioral finance concepts, such as regret avoidance, and simply talking about client fears is one way to use the "third ear" to pay attention to what a client is really saying so that an effective response can be made.

TRANSFERENCE AND COUNTERTRANSFERENCE

At this point, it is important to consider two concepts that come into play during client–financial planner discussions. The first factor, *transference,* refers to the ways in which a client's feelings and communication patterns are affected by unfinished business or emotional baggage,[14] typically related to significant people in the client's past, such as parents or a previous financial adviser. *Countertransference* is similar, but on the part of the financial planner. All financial planners have conscious and unconscious feelings from their past that may be triggered by a client's words or behaviors. These feelings may hinder or help client–financial planner communication, but in either case, it is important to recognize when transference and countertransference is occurring within the communication process.

In transference, the client *transfers* their feelings associated with a past event or person to that of their financial planner, potentially disrupting and hindering the communication process. For example, a financial planner may say something to the client that sounds similar to what a disloyal past significant other or adviser once said. Subsequently, the client may experience feelings of distrust rush back in, even though on an intellectual level the client knows her current financial planner is a different person.

Consider a situation when a financial planner makes a neutral statement, but because of transference the client interprets the statement as criticism because he or she associates the statement (and now the financial planner) with another authority figure, such as an overly critical father. Dealing with adverse impacts of transference is discussed in greater depth in later chapters, but one of the best strategies is to ask a client about his or her past positive and negative experiences with family members, relationships, and other professionals regarding money issues and financial planning. This allows the financial planner to more easily identify when transference might be occurring.

In reaction to a client statement or behavior, a financial planner may also have emotional baggage that unconsciously clouds his judgment or affects his client communication. This is countertransference. A common countertransference reaction that gives financial planners trouble occurs when a financial planner becomes unusually frustrated by repeated action or inaction on the part of a client that is contradictory to the financial plan or financial planner's recommendations. A certain amount of frustration may be expected, but it is counterproductive if the financial planner then acts out of anger or frustration when communicating with the client. For example, consider a financial planner whose goal is to provide valuable advice that leads to improved client behaviors. If the client fails to act on these recommendations, and the financial planner reacts negatively, this is countertransference. As a financial planner, you will know this is occurring if you catch yourself thinking something like: "My worth depends on how effective I am in my job (an old message from a beloved teacher or parent), so if a client doesn't follow my advice, I am a failure."

Financial planners should be mindful of the countertransference threat to their communication with clients and can limit potential adverse effects by directly addressing emotional responses with clients using many of the communication techniques discussed in later chapters. We believe that so much negative client–financial planner communication can be avoided if financial planners were more aware of countertransference. A financial planner who is aware of this possibility, and has the ability to take a step back and view his relationships and communication patterns with clients more objectively and critically, will be in a better position to help clients. Exercises are provided in later chapters to help financial planners increase their awareness of transference from clients and self-awareness of potential countertransference.

PASSIVE VERSUS ACTIVE LISTENING AND RESPONDING

Listening, and the responses listening generates, can be either passive or active. Some communication experts refer to *passive listening* as *nondirective listening* and *active listening* as *directive listening*. Much of what has been discussed in this chapter has illustrated the use of active listening skills. For example, the use of body language, when done purposely, results from being attentive and responding in a nonverbal manner. It is also possible to respond verbally as a result of active listening. Consider the following dialog between a client and financial planner. Is the financial planner's response passive or active?

> Client: "I simply don't know if I should pull the trigger and purchase that foreclosure and turn it into a rental."
>
> Planner: "Okay."
>
> Client: "I know there is some upside to the deal, but I also know that the house is going to take a lot of work to renovate. I just don't know what to do."
>
> Planner: "So, you are conflicted."
>
> Client: "Absolutely."

If you answered "passive," you are correct. In effect, the financial planner listened to the client's concern and responded in a way that confirmed the client's fears. The response, however, was not directed at creating either psychological or behavioral change, nor was the response intended to solicit additional information. Here is the same conversation. In this example, though, the financial planner takes an active listening role that results in a different (that is, directed) response:

Client: "I simply don't know if I should pull the trigger and purchase that foreclosure and turn it into a rental."

Planner: "Why do you say that?"

Client: "I know there is some upside to the deal, but I also know that the house is going to take a lot of work to renovate. I just don't know what to do."

Planner: "I'll tell you what. You are not taking into account the tax benefits of the transaction. Remember, I've been saying all along that you need to find a way to shelter some income. It seems to me that adding some rental properties to your portfolio will provide very nice write-offs in terms of depreciation. What do think?"

Client: "I hadn't thought about it that way. Maybe taking the risk is worth it."

The primary difference between passive and active listening and responding deals with the intended outcome. If a financial planner's purpose is to create trust or to signal to a client that he or she is free to talk some more, a passive response is appropriate. If, on the other hand, the purpose of responding to what has been heard is to promote action or another response from a client, a more direct active response may be needed. It is important to remember, however, that the use of either a passive or active response technique should come only after listening to the client and interpreting what was and is being said. Examples of both passive and active listening and responding will be highlighted through the remainder of this book.

SILENCE: A STRESSFUL TIME FOR CLIENT AND FINANCIAL PLANNER

Think of a time when you may have asked a client or colleague a serious and important question and the other person sat in *silence*. What was your initial reaction to the silence? Was it one of frustration? That is, did you ask yourself, "Why isn't this person answering me?" Were you curious as to whether or not the person understood the question? How long was it before you jumped back into the conversation and either asked a new question or clarified the original query? Most people, not just financial planners, tend to be very impatient when it comes to questioning and answering, and listening. Typically, a response of silence generates frustration on the part of the person who asked the question. To eliminate the awkwardness of a silent situation, nearly all people jump right back into dialog. This, however, is often the wrong thing to do.

VIDEO 4D

Video 4D illustrates how a financial planner can deal with silence during a client–financial planner meeting. Notice also how the financial planner addresses the issue of an "I don't know" answer.

According to De Jong and Berg (2008),[15] silence on the part of a client, when responding to a question, may simply be the client's way of clarifying his or her thoughts. Silence may also indicate that the client is tired and needs a moment to focus. A silent response can sometimes indicate a negative reaction. It is possible that silence might represent anger or confusion about a question or comment. Either way, the silence is communicating something.

The key thing to remember is that silence is generally okay. Consider the types of questions that are typically generated during a client–financial planner meeting. Questions from the financial planner tend to be cognitively difficult and complex, which require a client to process information and respond in a meaningful way. Think about how long it often takes clients to answer the following question: "Please list and rank your top five financial goals." Few clients can immediately respond to this question. It takes time to think about the request, weigh alternatives, rank the choices made, and communicate back to the financial planner. Interestingly, financial planners tend to feel stress after about five seconds of silence. It would be difficult, however, for anyone who was not prompted beforehand to answer this question within five seconds. The important takeaway from this discussion is to allow the client time—*auditory space*—to answer questions.

How long should a financial planner remain silent? There is no easy answer to this question, but allowing a client 10 to 15 seconds to respond is totally acceptable. It is important for financial planners to use their intuition to adjust from this standard. For example, a client's body language or other forms of nonverbal communication may indicate that he or she was confused by the question. It is possible that the question asked was odd or unclear. To wait 10 seconds to correct this type of mistake would only serve to make the client nervous and likely frustrated. If the question was clear, yet difficult, however, it is acceptable to sit back and allow the client time to craft a response. Remember, clients are usually just as frustrated with silence as the financial planner might be. Clients will work hard to fill silence, so give the clients time to think, and let them talk.

RESPONDING TO "I DON'T KNOW"

When someone is faced with a challenging or awkward question that he or she does not want to answer he or she will sometimes sit in silence or answer with "I don't know." While an "I don't know" response may be a legitimate answer—for example, "I don't know how much I will receive in Social Security benefits—the response is often a way for a client to deflect providing a truthful response.

Clients respond to stress in two primary ways. First, they may confront the stressor directly (in this case, their financial planner) or second, they will look for ways to alter the communication process. Financial planners often place their clients under stress. If a client responds by confronting a stressful question head on, he or she will provide the financial planner with useful information. If the client deflects the question by saying, "I don't know" or something similar, he or she may be sending a clear message that he or she is looking to disengage from the planning process. This helps explain why very aggressive salespeople often talk with a lot of people but rarely have a high close rate with those they meet. People are generally too courteous to fight back against aggressive sales tactics. They look for ways instead to appear engaged, while holding no expectations of returning to the relationship.

How should a financial planner handle an "I don't know" response? Generally, financial planners interpret this response as a cue to jump in with a solution, suggestion, clarification, or observation. This response may be appropriate. For example, if a financial planner were to ask someone whether they preferred a Roth IRA to a traditional IRA, the typical client's response might certainly be, "I don't know." This would often be followed by the client asking, "Why do you ask?" or "What do you think?" In this example, the burden to clarify the question falls squarely on the shoulder of the financial planner.

There are other times, however, when a client simply uses "I don't know" as a *stalling tactic*. Think back to the illustration earlier in the chapter when a financial planner asked a client to prioritize his or her five most important financial goals. This is a cognitively difficult question to answer. The question also has many hidden meanings, at least when viewed from a client's point of view. For example, a client may censor or edit his or her response based on what he or she believes the financial planner wants to hear. Other clients may freeze because they cannot identify five goals. Others may not be able to limit their list to just five outcomes. In any of these situations, the client may respond by saying, "I don't know." This is not really a cue that the client is unable to identify goals, but rather is reluctant to voice a response. The "I don't know" response is a way to deflect the question back to the financial planner.

At this point, a financial planner has several options from which to choose in regard to a response. The easiest response to make is to reframe the question or to volunteer a goal example, such as, "Many of my clients rank retirement first, college funding second, and other things like vacations, second homes, and charitable giving among the top five." In general, financial planners should avoid volunteering lists like this, unless the client asks for specific examples. Why? The financial planner's response tends to anchor the client to a defined list of alternatives rather than freeing his or her thinking to include goals that really matter to the client. Another option of response includes sitting quietly for 10, 15, or 20 seconds. This will obviously cause tension and added stress. The client will feel stressed, but as De Jong and Berg (2008)[16] suggest, clients often surprise themselves when given extra quiet time to think of a response. A third option involves responding by stating something like, "Most clients find this to be a very difficult question. Take your time." If this approach is taken in response to "I don't know," it is important for the financial planner to remain silent for at least 10 more seconds. If (and this is highly unlikely) the client were to remain silent, the financial planner ought to reframe the question or ask other questions that lead back to the query.

SUMMARY

As noted throughout this chapter, one of foundational elements of exceptional interpersonal communication is listening. It is fair to suggest that among all of the skills needed to achieve success as a financial planner, none is as important as listening. The next chapter introduces another important communication skill: questioning.

CHAPTER APPLICATIONS

1. Which of the following is not a component of the listening process?
   a. Paying attention to the client
   b. Paying attention to what is heard
   c. Interpreting what is heard
   d. Offering observations on what is being said
2. Which of the following body language approaches would cause a client to react in a negative way?
   a. Keeping arms, hands, and legs open to the client
   b. Matching a client's facial expressions
   c. Leaning away from a client
   d. Leaning toward a client

3. Clues that what a client is saying may have a deeper meaning include having the client
   a. Redirect questions back to the planner
   b. Make a joke in response to a serious question
   c. Avoid answering a direct question
   d. All of the above

4. When a client responds with silence, this means the client could be
   a. Angry.
   b. Tired.
   c. Confused.
   d. A or b or c.

5. If a client were to respond to a question by sitting silently, how long should a financial planner wait before reframing the question?
   a. 10 to 15 seconds
   b. At least one minute
   c. Until the client says something
   d. The planner should not wait, but rather immediately reframe the question

6. If a financial planner listens to a client's concern and recognizes that concern but makes no attempt to change the way the client feels or acts, then the financial planner is engaged in which of type of listening?
   a. Active
   b. Directive
   c. Passive
   d. Neutral

7. What two levels of language do clients use when talking with a financial planner?
   a. Surface and deeper
   b. First ear and third ear
   c. Right and left
   d. Focused and distracted

8. How can a financial planner know if a client's words have a deeper meaning?
   a. The client avoids making a direct decision
   b. The client attempts to redirect a financial planner's question
   c. Both a and b
   d. None of the above

9. Kristy has been working with her client Nolan for nearly three years. Over that period of time, Kristy has provided Nolan with numerous specific recommendations. Nolan, however, has implemented only a few recommendations. Kristy is frustrated that Nolan fails to take her advice. If Kristy does not manage her feelings appropriately, she may introduce which of the following into conversations with Nolan?
   a. Transference
   b. Countertransference
   c. Dependency
   d. Passive ambivalence

10. Which of the following prompts would be appropriately used by a financial planner when a client responds to a question by saying, "I don't know"?
    a. "Give me a break. You obviously do know."
    b. "Okay, let's move on to another question."
    c. "Why won't you answer this simple question?"
    d. "This is a hard question. Take your time."

11. Visit a local coffee house. Find a table that provides viewing access to other tables and booths in the shop. Without listening to anyone's conversation, identify body language cues being sent by those in the coffee house while engaged in a conversation. When viewing the scene, ask yourself the following questions: (1) How many conversations appear to be taking place using positive body language? (2) Is anyone using negative body language? and (3) Does the tone and volume of each conversation seem to match the body language being used?

12. Ask a friend or colleague to sit with you for a few minutes. Tell the person that you want to have a brief conversation about a topic of interest to both of you. When you meet, start the conversation by saying something like, "Thanks for helping me out. What do you want to talk about?" The response may be something like, "I don't know," "I don't care," or "Whatever you want." Rather than responding immediately, sit silently for at least 10 seconds. How long does it take before your conversation partner responds verbally to your silence?

13. Everyone has body language tendencies when communicating (e.g., talking with one's hands, looking down, crossing one's arms, nodding, etc.), and these tendencies are often inconsistent with the intended message. Think about your own body language tendencies when communicating and describe them. How do your body language tendencies hinder or strengthen your communication with others?

NOTES

1. G. McGregor and R. S. White, *Reception and Response: Hearer Creativity and the Analysis of Spoken and Written Texts* (London: Routledge, 1990).
2. A. Ivey and N. Gluckerstern, *Basic Influencing Skills*, 2nd ed. (Amherst, MA: Microtraining Associates, 1984).
3. A. E. Ivey, *Intentional Interviewing and Counseling*, 2nd ed. (Pacific Grove, CA: Brooks-Cole, 1988).
4. Id.
5. M. L. Knapp, *Nonverbal Communication in Human Interaction* (New York: Holt, Rinehart & Winston, 1972).
6. C. D. Aronovitch, "The Voice of Personality: Stereotyped Judgments and Their Relation to Voice Quality and Sex of Speaker," *Journal of Social Psychology* 99 (1976): 207–220.
7. J. Sommers-Flanagan and R. Sommers-Flanagan, *Foundations of Therapeutic Interviewing* (Needham Heights, MA: Allyn & Bacon, 1993).

8. D. G. Myers, *Psychology*, 2nd ed. (New York: Worth, 1989).
9. M. R. Endsley, "Measurement of Situation Awareness in Dynamic Systems," *Human Factors* 37 (1995): 65–84.
10. Sommers-Flanagan and Sommers-Flanagan, *Foundations of Therapeutic Interviewing*.
11. Nearly all of the communication strategies discussed later in this book involve techniques to enhance attending actions.
12. W. H. Cormier and L. S. Cormier, *Interviewing Strategies for Helpers: Fundamental Skills and Cognitive Behavioral Interventions*, 2nd ed. (Monterey, CA: Brooks-Cole, 1991).
13. T. Reik, *Listening with the Third Ear* (New York: Farrar, Strauss & Company, 1948).
14. D. Hutchinson, *The Essential Counselor: Process, Skills, and Techniques* (Boston: Houghton-Mifflin, 2007).
15. P. De Jong and I. K. Berg, *Interviewing for Solutions*, 3rd ed. (Belmont, CA: Thomson Higher Education, 2008).
16. Id.

5

Questioning

INTRODUCTION

The previous chapter emphasized the importance of listening. The ability to listen to what a client is saying is the most important element within the communication process. Assuming a financial planner has mastered the art of listening, the ability to ask questions is arguably the second-most important element. Questioning is really a product of the listening process. Dillon[1] noted that a question communicates something in addition to what is being asked. For example, consider the following question that illustrates how *presuppositions* shape communication:

> "When was the last time you robbed a bank?"

The person who asks this question—assuming the question is a serious one—presupposes that the other person is, in fact, a bank robber. There is no way for someone to answer this question without self-incrimination. More importantly, however, is what the question and resulting answer communicates. For the person who is asked to respond, the question is laden with presuppositions of guilt and accusation. For the person asking the question, any answer presupposes guilt.

The problem with presuppositions is that unless the underlying assumption is true, both the question and answer will cloud the communication process. To produce meaningful results within the financial planning process, questions must proceed from an honest attempt to obtain information as a mechanism to help a client. This means that questions should be honest and without trickery. Stated another way, clients will evaluate the sincerity of a question—and the financial planner who asks the question—by assessing both the content of the question and the attitude of the questioner.

The process of asking questions within the context of financial planning is different from, say, questioning conducted by attorneys or physicians. Within the legal profession, for example, attorneys are counseled to rarely, if ever, ask questions in a cross examination in which they do not already have an answer. Physicians tend to focus questions as a means of discovery to quickly develop an intervention recommendation. Financial planners, on the other hand, are inclined to approach client–financial planner interactions using questions as a means of obtaining information that will not only assist with financial plan development but also deepen aspects of the client–financial planner relationship. In some respects, questioning methods that are designed to promote this outcome need to be developed from an emotionally honest perspective. Dillon[2] argued that there are eight presumptions for a standard inquiry, each of which is essential for use by financial planners when working with clients. The following eight questioner attitudes represent aspects of questioning that reflect *honest inquiry:*

1. Acknowledging that more is to be known by asking a question
2. Being puzzled by the consequences of not knowing answers
3. Needing to know more information to contextualize a discussion and develop recommendations
4. Desiring to know a client's truth or reality
5. Believing both the truth of (assumptions underlying) a question and the response to the question
6. Being confident that what is currently unknown can be known
7. Having the courage to ask for additional information
8. Resolving to better understand another person through questions and answers

The following discussion reviews some of the most widely used questioning techniques employed by financial planners. When based on the eight elements of honest inquiry, the following questioning approaches can prompt insightful answers from clients.

OPEN-ENDED QUESTIONS

The formation of questions when working with clients often occurs on a very intuitive level. There are many ways a question may be formed and asked. In general, questions can either be open-ended or closed-ended. The approach taken—either open or closed—provides a very specific form of guidance to a client in terms of answering freely or in a controlled manner.

Open-ended questions cannot be answered with a simple "yes" or "no" response.[3] These types of questions often begin with the following terms:

- When
- Why
- Who
- How
- Tell me
- Where
- What

If the purpose of a question is to solicit as much information as possible, an open-ended question ought to begin with either "how" or "what." For example, if a financial planner asks a client, "When did you file your taxes?" the answer may be, "On March 12th." However, had the financial planner asked, "How did you file your taxes?" or "What does your process of filing taxes look like?" the response will be more informative. The client might respond by saying something like: "I went to the tax preparer down the street in March; she took my paperwork and filed an electronic return with the IRS." Technically, both responses are open-ended, in that the client really could not respond using a "yes" or "no" answer, but the second answer was deeper, more informative, and generally more meaningful.

It is important to note that financial planners should be careful when framing questions with a "why" query. Clients often perceive a question that starts with "why" as being adversarial or even manipulative, which almost always results in a defensive response. Think about a time when someone asked you why you did or did not do something. What was your reaction? If you are like most people, your initial reaction was to answer in a self-protective way. Consider the following dialog:

Planner: "The last time we met, you indicated that you were going to increase contributions to your company's 401(k) plan. How did that go?"

Client: "I totally forgot about that."

Planner: "Why didn't you remember? You know, it was really important."

Client: "Yeah, you are right. My bad. Time just got away from me and I didn't make it to the payroll office."

In this example, the financial planner cornered the client by asking for justification to an activity that was not completed. The client could have responded in several ways, but to remain cordial, the client chose a diplomatic response that was somewhat apologetic. The question did not lead, however, to increasing the client's sense of empowerment or confidence. Here is how the planner could have better framed the question:

Planner: "The last time we met, you indicated that you were going to increase contributions to your company's 401(k) plan. How did that go?"

Client: "I totally forgot about that."

Planner: "Not a problem. When do you think you'll be able to meet with the folks in your human resources office?"

Client: "Probably this Friday."

Planner: "Let me know if you need any help, or even a reminder. Once you make that change you are going to see a big difference in your after-tax pay."

CLOSED-ENDED QUESTIONS

As suggested earlier, an open-ended question is one in which alternative choices are not explicitly indicated by the financial planner. On the other hand, a *closed-ended question* is structured in a manner that answers are specified by the financial planner. Closed-ended questions typically begin with one of the following terms:

- Are you . . .
- Do you . . .
- Is this . . .
- Is that . . .

Closed-ended questions should be used primarily to gather specific information needed during the financial planning process, whereas open-ended questions should be used to promote verbalization.[4] Consider the following example during a meeting between a financial planner and client. The financial planner is interested in learning about the client's preference when taking a financial risk. Here is how the dialog might unfold using an open-ended questioning method:

Planner: "So, Jerry, I would like to get your feelings about investment risk. As you know, when we establish an asset allocation model for clients, we try to match portfolio constraints to each client's investment preferences. I know this is a tough question, but tell me about your preferences when it comes to investing."

Client: "Oh, that is really a hard question. As I told you earlier, about ten years ago I dabbled in the stock market and lost a lot of money. My wife gave me a really hard time about that. Since then I've been a bit reluctant to jump back into risky investments. Lately, I have been buying gold coins. Last month I bought shares in a mining company, and the stock has been doing well. But, really I don't like to take too many risks. If you pressed me, I'd say I like to keep my money safe."

The following example illustrates how the financial planner might have asked the same question using a closed-ended questioning method:

Planner: "So, Jerry, I would like to get your feelings about investment risk. As you know, when we establish an asset allocation model for clients, we try to match portfolio constraints to each client's investment preferences. Let's say you had $100,000. Would you prefer to invest this money in (a) the stock market, (b) bonds, (c) diversified mutual funds, or (d) the bank?"

Client: "That is tough question, but given the choices, I will go with the bank."

VIDEO 5A AND 5B

Video 5A illustrates how a financial planner might ask an open-ended question. Be sure to note how freely the client responds and what type of information is volunteered.

Video 5B demonstrates the use of a closed-ended question technique. Notice how the financial planner uses the question to control the type of response offered by the client.

What is interesting about these examples is that Jerry—the client—answered both questions honestly. However, his response to each question could easily lead to conflicting conclusions about his risk preference. Using the open-ended question, the financial planner learned that Jerry's perception of what is or is not risky probably does not match definitional frameworks used by most financial planners. Few planners, for example, would equate purchasing gold coins and mining stocks as equivalent to putting one's money in the bank. Coins and mining stocks have low liquidity and sometimes limited marketability. The price of mining stocks can be quite volatile. Bank deposits, on the other hand, provide guaranteed and insured returns with high liquidity. Information about Jerry's definitional framework, experience, and history were totally missed using the closed-ended questioning method. Within the context of the closed-ended method, the financial planner might assume that Jerry holds a very risk-averse attitude, when, in fact, his preferences for risk taking appear to be more eclectic.

CHOOSING BETWEEN OPEN AND CLOSED-ENDED QUESTIONS

In general, open-ended questioning generates the least complete, but the most accurate, information. Closed-ended questioning results in the least accurate but most complete information. Implications resulting from this insight may not be intuitive. Rather than stating one form of questioning as superior to another, it is more appropriate to conclude that both methods can lead to useful information when used appropriately.

For example, assume a financial planner is attempting to narrow a diverse set of choices from many to a few as way to focus a client on a decision framework. A closed-ended questioning technique will likely produce a more favorable outcome. That is, selecting choices and asking a client to choose from those selected can help a client identify a product or service that best matches his or her feelings. Of course, this assumes that the choice selections are appropriate and suitable.

There are times, however, when the purpose of questioning is not necessarily to drive a client toward a choice decision. Financial planners often want to encourage their clients to think freely, with few imposed controls, as a way to learn how a client prefers to express him- or herself. This concept is related to *preferred communication styles* (for example, auditory, visual, kinesthetic). Much can be learned about a person's preferred communication style by allowing them to talk freely and openly. Consider the following client–financial planner discussion:

> Client: "I definitely see what you are saying. When I view the world, I think that if I had the right connections and insights, I could make some serious money in the markets."
>
> Planner: "What would you do if you made a lot of money in the markets?"
>
> Client: "That is an easy one. I can see myself on an island. Maybe it is Tahiti or even somewhere in the Caribbean. Imagine those ocean views. I would just relax and enjoy every day. Do you see what I mean? Man, if I only had the money…"

Although the financial planner, in this example, did not say much, she likely learned a lot about her client, simply by allowing the client to freely think and talk about the topic. The financial planner learned that the client has a primary *visual* communication and learning style. The client's use of terms like "see" and "view," were giveaways in this regard.

Using these cues, the financial planner would be well served to then adopt the same communication style and language with her client. Saying something simple like "I see what you mean," would be an ideal way to keep the dialog moving forward. A client who uses phrases like "I hear what you mean," "That resonates with me," and "That sounds like a good idea" most likely prefers an *auditory* communication style. Someone who says something like, "I just don't get it" or "I don't feel like that would be a good investment" probably has a *kinesthetic* communication preference.

QUESTION TRANSFORMATIONS

It is important to take care when formulating both open and closed-ended questions. It is very easy to fall into a questioning trap. Consider a situation in which a financial planner and client are discussing a topic like financial risk tolerance. The financial planner might ask a question like, "How did you feel when you lost money in the stock market the first time?" This is an open-ended question that will prompt the client to disclose information. What happens, however, when the financial planner asks, "How did you feel when you lost money in the stock market for the first time—did you lose sleep at night?" What was an appropriate open-ended question turned into a closed-ended question with the addition of the planner's response limitation ("did you lose sleep at night?"). This is called a *question transformation*.

Transforming open-ended questions to closed-ended question should be avoided. Why? The addition of the transformative statement limits the client's ability to answer freely. The client may also feel as if the financial planner is attempting to steer the answer in one direction or another.

VIDEO 5C

Video 5C shows how the use of swing questions can be used to solicit information from a client in which the client and financial planner have a good working rapport.

SWING QUESTIONS

Financial therapists often rely on swing questions to elicit information from clients. A *swing question* is a closed-ended question that generally prompts a client to reveal more than a simple "yes" or "no" answer. Questions that begin with words such as "will," "can," "could," or "would" allow someone to answer succinctly while offering an opportunity to contribute more information.[5] The following are examples of swing questions that might be asked during a client–financial planner meeting:

- "Will you give me an idea of how much is in the account?"
- "Could you call your real estate agent tomorrow and ask about what additional information is needed on the disclosure statement?"
- "Can you tell me a bit more about your employer-provided disability insurance plan?"
- "Would you be willing to visit with our estate attorney next Wednesday?"

The use of swing questions is encouraged, with the following caveats.[6] First, you should avoid swing questions during initial client–financial planner interactions or during client information meetings. Swing questions should be asked only when rapport has already been established between a client and a financial planner. Unless open dialog has been established, it is possible that a prospective client will respond in a closed manner (yes or no) to a swing question. For example, a financial planner might ask a client if she would be willing to meet with an attorney. The client could answer with an effortless "no," in which case the financial planner would be forced to use another questioning method to obtain additional information or to prompt action. Second, swing

questions should be avoided whenever a client appears to be opposi-
tional or not favoring a recommended implementation approach. Asking
a swing question in these situations can generate an answer that closes
the door to further discussion.

IMPLIED AND PROJECTIVE QUESTIONS

Financial planners often use two other forms of questions when working
with clients. The first is known as an *implied* or *indirect question*. As was
the case with swing questions, implied questioning should be used only
when the client–financial planner relationship is already well established.
By its very nature, an implied question solicits information in a rounda-
bout manner, typically by asking "I wonder" or "you must." For example,
a financial planner might ask, "I wonder what your plans are when you
retire." This is an indirect way of asking, "What do you plan to do when
you retire."

VIDEO 5D AND 5E

Video 5D illustrates the use of an implied questioning technique. Notice how the financial planner shows a sincere interest in the client's
ideas and answers.

Video 5E shows how a projective question can be incorporated
into a client–financial planner discussion. In this example, the financial
planner uses the technique to learn more about the client's feelings and
values and how the use of swing questions can be used to solicit more
information.

The second type of question is known as a *projective inquiry.* Projective
questioning methods originated in the context of psychotherapy to request
or solicit unconscious thoughts, values, and feelings from patients. Whenever
a question begins with words like "what if," "if you," or "what would" it is
safe to assume that the question is projective. The most common example
of a projective question is as follows: "If you had three wishes, what would
you wish for?" An illustration from a financial planning session includes the
following: "If you could go forward in time, what legacy would you like to
be remembered for among your friends, family, and colleagues?" Answers
to these types of questions allow a client to visualize, and to some extent,
articulate their life dreams.

SCALING QUESTIONS

Although not widely used by financial planners, scaling questions are among the most effective ways to help clients contextualize their ideas, perceptions, hopes, dreams, and fears. *Scaling questions* are also very useful in helping a client gauge their current progress toward meeting future financial objectives and goals. The development and use of scaling questions comes most directly from the work of de Shazer (1988)[7] and Berg and de Shazer (1993),[8] who introduced the mental health fields to the concept of solution-focused counseling techniques. Basically, a scaling question asks clients to indicate their impression, observation, prediction, or other response on a scale, which is typically from zero to 10 or 1 to 10. Consider the following example:

> Planner: "Sheri, I am so glad to see you again today. When our meeting was over last week, you indicated that you were feeling confident about your financial future. On a scale of 1 to 10, with 1 being totally not confident and 10 being absolutely confident, you indicated a score of 7. This week, you've brought in your tax records. I wonder, after going through all your records, notes, and receipts, how are you feeling about your financial situation? Let's use the same scale, only this time, let's make 1 mean totally uneasy and 10 mean totally at ease."
>
> Client: "That is an easy one. I would say, right now, I am feeling about 5 on that scale."

According to De Jong and Berg (2008),[9] scaling questions offer great versatility because they help clients articulate concerns, aspects of behavioral change, and willingness to engage in new activities in a relatively nonthreatening manner. Caution is warranted, however, with the use of scaling questions. Consider again the discussion from before. Sheri—the client—indicated feeling only somewhat at ease with her financial situation after getting her tax records ready for the financial planner. It would be easy for her financial planner to respond as follows:

> Planner: "That is interesting but not surprising. Tell me, how come so low and not, say, a 6, 7, or 8?"

While this question, in response to a scaling answer, may seem totally reasonable, financial planners are cautioned against using this type of retort. Instead, the financial planner could have asked the following question:

> Planner: "That is interesting but not surprising. Tell me, how come your score was so high?"

This reaction to Sheri's response is both encouraging and thought provoking. Similar to appreciative inquiry, reframing the response this way helps the client focus on positive events and outcomes. Consider Sheri's response and the ongoing dialog here:

> Client: "I thought you were going to be annoyed when I answered, '5.' After all, last week I was feeling pretty good about things. This week I'm not quite as confident. Anyway, I guess what you are saying is that I don't need to worry too much. A 5 is not too bad."
>
> Planner: "You are absolutely correct. A 5 is fine. In fact, it is pretty high, considering all the stress involved with tax planning. I am interested, though, as to why you are not, say, a 4."
>
> Client: "I am not a 4 because I know that you are here to help me. I am not feeling so alone in terms of my finances and taxes."

> **VIDEO 5F**
>
> Video 5F highlights the use of scaling questions. Notice how encouraging the financial planner responds to the client. The planner is intentionally attempting to give credence to the client's perceptions, while also attempting to solicit useful information that can be incorporated into the planning process.

Scaling questions, as this example illustrates, can be used with almost every client and in nearly every type of client–financial planner interaction. The way in which a financial planner frames each question can lead to deeper conversations about goal formation, recommendation implementation, and formalizing the client–financial planner relationship. Also, through the use of scaling questions, a financial planner can help a client move "up the ladder" in the sense of scores on the scale. In one of the earlier examples, it is likely that Sheri, over time, will increase her score from 5 to 6 to 7 or higher. By having Sheri verbalize her score and describe why she is not lower, the financial planner reinforces the positive impact of the planning process and the effectiveness of ongoing client–financial planner interactions.

SUMMARY

Questions, within the context of financial planning, generate both answers and reactions among clients. Some reactions are positive. Other reactions are negative. It is important for financial planners to prepare their questioning methods carefully, implement questioning appropriately, and continually monitor their clients' responses to certain questioning methods as a way to enhance client–financial planner interactions. Regardless of the type of question, financial planners should follow the following questioning guidelines, as outline by Sommers-Flanagan and Sommers-Flanagan[10] in their seminal text on therapeutic interviewing:

1. Let clients know, up front, how each session will be structured. This means informing clients that they will be asked one or more questions.
2. Although a series of questions may have been developed, the client's responses should direct the flow of conversation. That is, it is imperative for each financial planner to use his or her listening skills as the primary tool when questions are asked.
3. Relate questions directly to each client's needs and circumstances. Another way of saying this is to stay centered and focused on the client.
4. Use questions to both solicit information and to help clients focus on aspects of the financial planning process.
5. Be careful when exploring sensitive areas with clients. What may not seem particularly sensitive or important to a financial planner may be delicate to a client. Questions related to socioeconomic status, gender preference, individual and family difficulties, and other similar topics should be presented with care and empathy.

CHAPTER APPLICATIONS

1. A financial planner who wants to control a client–financial planner meeting through the use of questions should use:
   a. Open-ended questions
   b. Closed-ended questions
   c. Scaling questions
   d. Implied questions

2. A question that can be answered with a "yes" or "no" response but also leads to deeper discussions is known as a(n):
   a. Open-ended question
   b. Scaling question
   c. Swing question
   d. Projective question

3. "If you could develop a new tax system, what would it look like?" is an example of a(n):
   a. Projective question
   b. Swing question
   c. Implied question
   d. Scaling question

4. During a client–financial planner meeting the financial planner senses that the client is feeling stressed about her financial situation. The planner would like to gauge how stressed the client is feeling. Given this objective, which of the following questioning strategies would be most appropriate in addressing the planner's objective?
   a. Asking a projective question
   b. Asking a closed-ended question
   c. Asking an implied question
   d. Asking a scaling question

5. A financial planner asks her client the following question: "Will you allow me to merge your two accounts for reporting purposes?" This is an example of a(n):
   a. Open-ended question
   b. Swing question
   c. Projective question
   d. Implied question

6. Instead of asking, "When do you plan to purchase a vacation home" a financial planner might ask, "I wonder what your vacation plans in the future look like." This second question is an example of a(n):
   a. Closed-ended question
   b. Swing question
   c. Projective question
   d. Implied question

7. Aman asks each of his clients the following question: "At the end of our meeting today, what are two outcomes you hope to accomplish?" This is an example of a(n):
   a. Open-ended question
   b. Swing question
   c. Projective question
   d. Implied question

8. When following up a scaling question, which is the appropriate technique?
   a. "Tell me why you are so low on the scale."
   b. "Tell me why aren't you a 7 instead of a 5 on the scale."

    c. "Tell me why your score is so high."

    d. "Tell me what it is going to take to get you to a 10 on the scale."

9. Open-ended questions allow a client to provide more information. Which of the following open-ended questions is most likely to be interpreted by a client as manipulative?

    a. "Why didn't you increase your 401(k) contributions?"

    b. "How are you feeling about your portfolio's performance?"

    c. "When would you like to meet again?"

    d. "Where might you prefer to live when you retire?"

10. The best type of question:

    I. Helps a client focus on aspects of their financial plan.

    II. Helps a financial planner solicit information.

    III. Helps a financial planner keep the flow of conversation moving.

       a. II only

       b. I and II

       c. II and III

       d. I, II, and III

11. Match the following question words with the type of question the word best represents[12]:

1. What	a. Open
2. I wonder . . .	b. Closed
3. Why	c. Swing
4. Do you . . .	d. Implied
5. Did you . . .	e. Projective
6. Could you . . .	
7. How	
8. What if . . .	

12. Working with a classmate or colleague, develop two question examples for the following types of questioning techniques:

    a. Open

    b. Closed

    c. Implied

    d. Projective

    e. Swing

13. Find a partner (a classmate or colleague) and ask the person if he or she is willing to have a brief discussion. Choose a topic that is of interest to your partner (note: the topic can be anything from sports to financial planning). Begin your questioning by asking a series of closed-ended questions. After two or three questions, change your questioning approach to a combination of open and swing inquiries. Based on your discussion, answer the following questions: (a) Did your partner respond more or less favorably to the closed-ended question? (b) Which questioning approach provided the most information? and (c) Which questioning method put your partner the most at ease?

14. Ask a friend, colleague, or classmate if he or she is willing to answer a few questions about a current issue or topic in the news. Once you find someone who is willing to have a short chat, formulate a scaling question around the topic. For example, you might ask, "On a scale of 0 to 10, with 0 being absolutely disagree and 10 being totally agree, how do you feel about increasing the capital gains tax rate on dividends?" Follow this scaling question by asking the other person, "Why so high on the scale?" Based on his or her response, do you feel the scaling question provides useful information about his or her attitude on an issue or topic?

15. Think about the interaction between the use of silence discussed in the previous chapter and the use of questions discussed in this chapter. When you are asked questions, how quickly do you generally feel you need to respond? Most people say that in a typical conversation they try to quickly respond. A client will generally feel the same way, particularly if he or she receives messaging from a financial planner who is uncomfortable with silence. Use of silence and use of questions are both invaluable communication skills that interact. Please describe how they can be used together to elicit the most valuable information from clients and build a strong rapport.

16. The next time you're in a social situation with friends or family or at a social event, spend some time observing the interactions between people. Participate in the conversation as much as necessary to avoid drawing negative attention, but focus most of your energy on the observation of the questions asked and reactions of people who are asked questions. Note which questions seemed to be the most helpful to the conversation and those that appeared to draw less positive emotions or hinder the dialog and vice versa. An important part of the process of becoming an effective communicator and financial planner is related to you developing a strong capacity to observe and learn from those observations.

NOTES

1. J. T. Dillion, *The Practice of Questioning: International Series on Communication Skills* (London: Routledge, 1990).
2. J. T. Dillion, "Student Questions and Individual Learning," *Educational Theory* 36 (1986): 333–341.
3. J. Sommers-Flanagan and R. Sommers-Flanagan, *Foundations of Therapeutic Interviewing* (Needham Heights, MA: Allyn & Bacon, 1993).
4. According to Sommers-Flanagan and Sommers-Flanagan (1993), it is relatively easy to change a closed-ended question to an open-ended question, and vice versa. For example, instead of asking, "Do you understand how a tax exchange works?" it might be more helpful to ask, "How would you explain a tax exchange to someone to my para-planner?" The first question can be answered either "yes" or "no," while the second question can only be answered with an in-depth verbalization.

5. S. C. Shea, *Psychiatric Interviewing: The Art of Understanding* (Philadelphia: W. B. Saunders, 1988).
6. Sommers-Flanagan and Sommers-Flanagan, *Foundations of Therapeutic Interviewing.*
7. S. de Shazer, *Clues: Investigating Solutions in Brief Therapy* (New York: Norton, 1988).
8. I. K. Berg and S. de Shazer, "Making Numbers Talk: Language in Therapy," in *The New Language of Change: Constructive Collaboration in Psychotherapy,* ed. S. Friedman (New York: Guilford Press, 1993).
9. P. De Jong and I. K. Berg, *Interviewing for Solutions,* 3rd ed. (Belmont, CA: Thomson Higher Education, 2008).
10. Sommers-Flanagan and Sommers-Flanagan, *Foundations of Therapeutic Interviewing.*

6

Nondirective Communication

Imagine a continuum like the one shown in Figure 6.1. This is a visual representation of how those working in the counseling professions differentiate between a client and a helping professional (financial planner) being at the center of a discussion or meeting.[1] On the top side of the continuum are clients. Communication techniques used here are intended to elicit attitudinal and behavioral information, and to promote open dialog and discussion between the client and financial planner. The bottom side of the continuum shows the financial planner–focused side of communication. As the focus of communication moves from top to bottom, the emphasis changes from client-centered discussion to communication that is directed by the adviser as a means of influencing behavior.

Here is an easy way to conceptualize what is going on in the figure: *nondirectional communication* is designed to encourage clients to talk and open up about their financial dreams, aspirations, and hoped-for life outcomes. *Directive communication* is much more focused on leading clients to a solution.

Much of what has been discussed in this book, up until this point, has dealt with nondirective communication strategies and approaches. For example, the use of silence and scaling questions exemplify nondirective communication methods. These types of techniques are used almost exclusively to facilitate client–financial planner discussions. Counselors and therapists sometimes call these communication techniques *attending behavior*.

Nondirectional: Client
Centered

Directive: Planner
Centered

FIGURE 6.1 The Continuum of Communication

This chapter provides more examples of nondirective communication. A discussion about directive communication is presented in the next chapter. As described next, this sequencing is purposeful.

Nearly all financial planners have been educated to use directive communication strategies. This makes sense because financial planners usually think in a directive manner. That is, there is a tendency among those in the profession to view the act of seeking help as a signal that a client not only wishes, but needs to, change something in his or her financial life. Therefore, financial planning professionals and related advisers expect their staff to act as an expert who has been hired to steer a client toward a financial solution. This fits well, in fact, with some elements of the financial planning process. Of the key steps in the process, conducting an analysis, making a recommendation, and implementing strategies are all directive in nature. It is during these steps in the financial planning process that a financial planner uses her expertise, knowledge, and professional judgment to guide a client toward an optimal financial solution to meet one or more client objectives or issues. Some, in fact, might argue that this really is the essence of financial planning.

Financial planners, as a group of professionals, tend to be very goal and action-oriented. Financial planners, based on their preferences and education, are also often very solution driven. Consider a typical weekend radio talk show in which a financial planner helps answer callers' financial questions. Given the nature of talk radio, the announcer has only a few seconds to obtain information from a caller. Furthermore, the announcer must gather and synthesize information quickly and develop a solution that is both timely and entertaining enough to keep all listeners engaged. Within this pressure-packed environment, financial planners who have a radio show tend to work very well at developing and presenting solutions to problems.

While this ability to react quickly and efficiently process information that leads to the development of solutions is an asset, this skill is only valuable if the information obtained is of high quality. If the information a financial planner uses to develop a solution is flawed or incomplete, the resulting plan, recommendation, or implementation strategy will likely be less than optimal. In fact, plan failure may be quite likely. As such, it is imperative that financial planners, regardless of where their preference may fall on the continuum of communication, have a strong grasp of nondirective communication techniques. When viewed from the perspective of the financial planning process, nondirective communication is most closely aligned with establishing the client–financial planner relationship, gathering data, and monitoring a client's plan on an ongoing basis. It is precisely how well a financial planner can promote *open dialog* among his or her clientele at these three points in the financial planning process that drives client trust and commitment.

WHY NONDIRECTIVE COMMUNICATION?

The role of nondirective communication has been highlighted throughout this book. Think back to earlier discussions about attending behavior. The use of nonverbal communication techniques, like making eye contact, nodding appropriately, and mirroring a client's bodily behavior, was presented as a way to promote client engagement and trust. Other aspects of nondirective communication include the effective use of silence and basic questioning approaches. The purpose of nondirective communication, as simple as it may seem, is to make discussing financial topics with clients easier.

Sometimes, aspiring financial planners, as well as those with many years of experience, find nondirective communication too time consuming and cumbersome. Some financial planners are anxious and eager to learn about a client's problem and jump into the development of problem solutions. This is especially true among new financial planners. This makes sense and may, in fact, be appropriate if a client's presenting issue[2] can be easily identified and analyzed. Unfortunately, this is rarely the case. Consider the following situation.

During an uptrend period in the markets, a married couple sought the help of a financial planner. During the opening minutes of the first client–financial planner meeting, the husband indicated that he and his wife wanted to begin investing in the stock market. The financial planner listened attentively, used nonverbal communication techniques efficiently, and noted what he identified as the goal of the client. Based on this assessment, he opened the client file and noted that both the husband and wife had completed the firm's risk-tolerance assessment, as well as other data-gathering forms. Besides introductory remarks and introductions, the total amount of time spent on nondirectional communication was, perhaps, 30 minutes. Based on the apparent facts, the financial planner set to work developing a model portfolio that would help his new clients attain their stated goal.

This story is not uncommon in financial planning practice. In fact, the financial planner in this case was one of the authors at the beginning of his career. It turns out that while the husband was entirely correct in stating that he and his wife wanted to begin investing in the stock market, and that they reported a willingness to take a reasonable amount of risk when implementing this goal, the clients really had an entirely different set of goals in mind, none of which, by the way, were disclosed during the meeting. Here is what the wife wanted to say but did not:

"Every day my husband goes to work and listens to his buddies talk about how much money they are making in the stock market. When he comes home, he gets depressed because all of our money is in the bank. Since interest rates have been falling, our quarterly income from interest has been going down. So, we are 'losing' money when everyone else is making money! What should we be doing now?"

This is the type of information that can be obtained when nondirectional communication techniques are used effectively. This is also an example of the important information a financial planner needs to know to help a client maximize financial outcomes. While it is possible that developing an efficient portfolio might address these clients' underlying concerns, here is what actually happened: during the next bear market this married couple pulled out of the stock market entirely (at the bottom) and did not move money back into equities for several years. In retrospect, almost all of the financial stress felt by this couple could have been minimized had nondirectional communication strategies been used more effectively during the data-gathering phase of the financial planning process.

What did the financial planner (one of the authors) do wrong in this example? Looking back, as authors who have studied communication techniques, we can see that the financial planner was anxious to produce results for these clients. Rather than focus on exploring feelings related to goal motivation, the young planner interpreted the husband's stated outcome as synonymous with expecting high relative portfolio performance. In turns out that while the clients did expect decent performance, they were most interested in balancing safety with the comfort of knowing that, when compared to their co-workers and friends, they were being smart with their money. This goal is not the same as asking a financial planner to construct an alpha-generating efficient portfolio. If a time machine existed, we would go back and instruct our younger self to "use nondirective communication techniques more effectively" because these provide a platform, when combined with attending behavior, to learn what is really driving a client's questions and needs.

OUTCOMES ASSOCIATED WITH NONDIRECTIVE COMMUNICATION

What is it that a financial planner needs to know during the client engagement and data-gathering phases of the planning process? From a broad perspective, one key piece of information is whether the adviser believes that the client–financial planner relationship will flourish in the future. Stated another way, the financial planner needs to be fairly confident that the client fits well with the financial planner's practice. Nondirective communication techniques are an excellent way for a financial planner to determine this fit. On a much more practical level, the adviser must obtain high-quality information about a client's current financial behavior, anticipated behavior, attitudes, and emotions. This information is not always easy to obtain. The good news is that nondirective communication strategies can be used to better understand how clients think about and interact with money and personal finance topics.

On the surface, most financial planning topics appear to be very quantitative in nature. For example, developing a portfolio allocation, withdrawal rate, and retirement income distribution strategy for someone entering retirement can be conducted purely from a spreadsheet point of view. This does not mean, however, that portfolio recommendations or other strategies will necessarily be implemented or that the client will adjust his or her future behavior to match a plan's underlying assumptions. This is the reality of financial planning. The best conceptualized plans are worth very little unless a client both implements and maintains a financial planner's recommendations. Much of the academic literature that addresses financial decision making indicates that financial planners who focus primarily on the technical or quantitative nature of the financial planning process may, in fact, be missing an important element associated with future plan implementation. Understanding how clients view money, the financial landscape, and financial markets is just as important when developing long lasting client–financial planner relationships as clarifying technical assumptions and inputs.

Obtaining *emotional evidence* about a particular client is a primary outcome associated with nondirective communication approaches. In the mid-1970s, Izard[3] identified 10 distinct or primary emotions exhibited by clients going through counseling. The following emotions encompass the way nearly all clients view aspects of financial planning. These emotions also describe how financial planners feel about the choices their clients make in relation to plan implementation decisions:

1. Joy
2. Excitement
3. Surprise
4. Distress
5. Anger
6. Disgust
7. Contempt
8. Fear
9. Shame
10. Guilt

While it may make some financial planners nervous to think about how emotionally connected clients become to money issues, it is nonetheless important for financial planners to acknowledge that emotions drive nearly all financial decisions.[4]

Consider again the story of the married couple discussed earlier who wanted to begin investing in the stock market. The young financial planner was intuitive enough to recognize that his clients were seeking help, in part, because of an emotional need. The problem was that he confused the husband's request for greater returns as an emotional cue that he and his wife were looking for investments that were a bit more exciting than what they currently owned and that they want to buy stocks as a way to generate higher returns. While excitement might have been one of the emotions held by the clients, it is apparent, in retrospect, that distress, fear, and guilt were also present in the situation. Had the financial planner taken a bit more time to delve deeper into the client's attitudes and emotions regarding money and investing, he may very well have uncovered the wife's fear of loss and the husband's shame at feeling less competent than his co-workers. This information certainly would have influenced both the type of portfolio developed and the ongoing level of client education undertaken by the financial planner.

VIDEO 6A

Video 6A illustrates how a financial planner can incorporate a summary statement and question into a client–financial planner discussion.

The remainder of this chapter describes four nondirectional communication techniques that can be used by any financial planner. Once a financial planner masters the use of clarification, summarization, reflection, and paraphrasing, the financial planner will begin to gain valuable insights into each client's behavioral tendencies, attitudes, and emotions.

CLARIFICATION

Clarification is the most basic form of nondirective communication. Clarification is used to recheck something a client says or does. This can be accomplished by saying something like:

"I want to make sure that I heard that correctly. Can you restate what you just said?"

Although clarification is a useful tool, caution is warranted to ensure that this technique is not overused. Asking a client to repeat what he or she has just said throughout a client–financial planner session can backfire. While it is true that the financial planner may be obtaining additional information, the client may perceive that the planner is not listening appropriately to what is being said. This can reduce client trust and commitment.

Sommers-Flanagan and Sommers-Flanagan[5] advocated a more complex form of clarification. They recommended the use of a double-questioning technique, which they described as "a restatement imbedded in a double question" (p. 66). Here is an example of a *double question:*

> Planner: "Did you sell the shares before or after the news broke in the *Journal of Financial Planning?*"

Let's revisit the situation with the young financial planner who was working with a married couple. Consider how a double question clarification might have helped the financial planner learn more about his clients' desire to begin investing in the stock market. He could have asked the clients something like:

> "Is what's driving you to think about stocks simply higher returns or is it something else?"

A question like this might have solicited a response from the wife indicating that the choice to move from relatively low-risk assets into higher-risk securities was a result of many factors, only one of which was the need for higher returns.

SUMMARIZATION

It is quite common for a keynote speaker to say something like, "Let me summarize," or "In summary…" after completing a speech or presentation. Unlike a speech, within the counseling and financial planning process, summarizations usually occur after a client has finished talking. A *summary statement* is a tool that can be used to clarify a client's goals and wishes. What makes a summary so confusing is that summarizing is often confused with paraphrasing, which is discussed later in the chapter. So, what exactly is a summary statement?

A summary statement is a brief summary of the content shared in a dialog.[6] A *paraphrase,* on the other hand, occurs when someone restates what someone else said. Here is an example of an effective summary statement based on the example from earlier in the chapter:

> Planner: "I want to make sure that I fully understand your concerns. What I'm hearing is that you are worried about falling interest rates and the impact that this is having on your portfolio. You are also now wanting to move from cash to stock investments. Does that pretty much cover what we have been talking about?

The use of a summary statement like this one will result in one of two primary client responses. The first is something like this: "Yes, that is right on target." The second response will be marked by client confusion or clarification. Looking back on the married couple's situation from earlier in the chapter, the use of this type of summary statement probably would have elicited a response similar to this one:

> Husband: "Yeah, that sounds about right."
>
> Wife: "Hold on a minute. I would say that is mostly correct, but not completely."
>
> Planner: "What do you mean?"
>
> Wife: "I think we know that we should probably be moving money from the bank into the stock market, but if truth be told, that makes me really nervous."
>
> Planner: "Okay, this is really helpful. In addition to needing higher returns, you are also nervous about the risks associated with the stock market. Does that sound right?"
>
> Wife: "Yes, that is correct."
>
> Husband: "I thought that is what I have been saying all along."

As this example illustrates, a summary statement can be used during multiple stages of a client–financial planner dialog. An easy way to think about a summary statement is to equate it with listing back to the client the key points made during the dialog. Rather than say something like, "Let me summarize. First, you want to increase returns. Second, you are interested in stocks, and third, you are worried about risk," it is generally a better idea to remain a bit more informal. While it is true that a summary is a listing of key points, making a formal or specific list can box both the financial planner and client into discussing issues that may or may not be relevant to the situation. Informal lists also keep clients engaged and thinking about what was not said, which makes future discussion more collaborative. The best advice regarding summary statements is probably this: be supportive of the client.[7]

REFLECTION

As discussed previously, much of what a client and financial planner discuss during meetings is emotionally charged. *Emotional responses* to financial planning questions, concerns, and issues are laden with sensitivities primarily because money issues tend to elicit thoughts of excitement, distress, anger, fear, and sometimes shame and guilt. When attempting to build rapport with a client, it is especially important to connect with the client emotionally. It would be quite odd, if not uncomfortable, for a financial planner to sit in an entirely detached manner as a client talks emotionally about his or her financial goals and dreams. Perhaps a client is upset that he did not receive a year-end bonus. While the bonus itself may not affect the client's long-term financial plan, the thought that his performance was deemed subpar by someone working in his firm may generate anger and suspicion, or even concern about job security. Here is how a reflection technique can be used in this type of emotionally charged situation:

> Client: "I am so angry. You cannot even begin to comprehend how mad I am at this moment. I was expecting that year-end bonus, and it just did not happen. My numbers were good and I thought I was well liked. I can tell you right now I am about to quit. I simply cannot stay at a firm that disrespects my efforts."
>
> Planner: "I have never seen you so angry. You are really mad."
>
> Client: "You know it."

VIDEO 6B

Video 6B demonstrates the use of a reflection statement by a novice financial planner. In this example, the reflection statement was not received well by the client. This is a result of the approach taken by the

(continued)

(*Continued*)

planner. Rather than reflecting back, with sincerity, the client's emotion, the planner's reflection attempt was unnatural. Notice also the inappropriate use of nonverbal communication techniques.

Notice that the financial planner's response is not a clarification or summary of the situation. The reflection statement simply and directly reflects the client's emotional language. The client in this situation used words like "angry" and "mad." The financial planner responded using the same terms. This situation is so emotionally charged that the financial planner could quickly find herself in trouble if she attempted to probe deeper or to interpret the anger in one way or another. Her use of the reflection technique was designed to let the client know that he was being heard and that she understands his anger. This can be an effective way to create closeness between a client and financial planner. It is, after all, difficult to be upset with someone who feels your pain.

As with all communication tools and techniques, it is possible to overuse or use reflection statements ineffectively. For example, financial planners are cautioned to always reflect back to the client what was said and to use the same intensity of voice. Responding with too much vigor to a mild form of emotion may prompt a client to question the financial planner's level-headed approach to planning. On the other hand, a reflection that is too mild may upset a client by implying that the financial planner is attempting to minimize the client's emotions. As such, reflection techniques should be used with caution and only by those financial planners who have a sincere appreciation for a client's feelings and concerns.

PARAPHRASING

Paraphrasing, which has been defined as "reflection or rephrasing of the content of what the client said"[8] is a very effective nondirective communication tool. As with other listening tracking skills, paraphrasing is most often used as a *confirmation* device. That is, clients learn, through financial planner paraphrasing (for example, restating what was said or rewording what was talked about), if the planner was hearing and interpreting the message. Paraphrasing plays another important role in the communication process. The act of restating helps clarify not only what a client said but what a client may have meant. This clarifying role helps move a discussion forward in a nondirective, and generally nonthreatening, manner.

> **VIDEO 6C**
>
> Video 6C demonstrates the use of a simple paraphrasing technique that conveys empathy toward a client.

The concept of paraphrasing is rather straightforward. There are several rules, however, associated with the technique. These are highlighted here:

1. Financial planners should use a restatement to echo the content of a client's message.
2. Paraphrasing should *not* be used to reflect a client's feelings.
3. Paraphrasing should *not* be employed to reflect a client's communication process.
4. Financial planners should keep their restatement brief and to the point.
5. Paraphrasing should *not* alter a client's point.
6. Paraphrasing should never add information that was not stated by a client.
7. Financial planners should be careful not to simply echo back exactly what a client said.

Point 7 from this list is important. Financial planners often think of paraphrasing as something too obvious to do on a regular basis. It is sometimes easy to think, "Well, of course, I heard the client. I don't really need to restate the obvious." Knowing that, however, as an effective communicator, a financial planner should be incorporating nondirective communication strategies into his or her dialog, aspiring and veteran financial planners sometimes make the mistake of repeating back, almost word for word, what a client just said. Consider the following example:

> Planner: "It looks like you have two really solid options in terms of making your purchase decision."
>
> Client: "Maybe so, but I am still not sure. On the one hand, I can take out a 30-year fixed rate mortgage, or I can opt for a five-year adjustable-rate mortgage. I really do not know which would be better."
>
> Planner: "You do not know which would be better."

The problem with this type of restatement is related to the message content. While the client certainly stated that she does not know which mortgage option to choose, the content of the message was more subtle. By simply restating back to the client her own words, the financial planner has done little to either clarify or confirm, in the mind of the client, the substance of the conversation. Consider the following alternative example:

Planner: "It looks like you have two really solid options in terms of making your purchase decision."

Client: "Maybe so, but I am still not sure. On the one hand I can take out a 30-year fixed rate mortgage, or I can opt for a five-year adjustable-rate mortgage. I really do not know which would be better."

Planner: "So, you are worried about making the wrong choice between a 30-year fixed rate and five-year adjustable-rate mortgage."

Although the length of the two paraphrasing approaches is nearly the same, the message conveyed back to the client is significantly different. Rather than being a somewhat rigid restatement, the second paraphrasing attempt reflects more accurately the client's worry and fear about the decision-making process. As a technique, the second example works better than the first attempt because it conveys empathy and support for the client.

STYLES OF PARAPHRASING

Paraphrasing techniques can be classified into one of three styles[9]: (1) simple, (2) sensory, and (3) metaphorical. As the style name implies, a *simple paraphrase* involves a restatement of content. Here is an example:

Planner: It is so nice to see you today.

Client: Nice to see you too.

Planner: When you called, it sounded like you had a question about insurance coverage?

Client: That is an understatement. I learned yesterday that I need to make a new health plan choice at work. I am scared that I will choose the wrong plan, and if I do, I might not be able to pay for my daughter's medical expenses this year.

> Planner: So, you are worried that you might make the wrong choice when choosing a health plan this year. Is that correct?
>
> Client: That's right. I am definitely worried.

VIDEO 6D

Video 6D illustrates how a financial planner can adapt multiple paraphrasing styles into a client–financial planner session.

During the video, identify at least two forms of paraphrasing. Also, does the client attempt to paraphrase what is communicated by the planner?

The use of *sensory paraphrasing* is based on the favored learning and communication style of clients. Recall from earlier chapters that clients generally have a preferred communication style. Nearly all people have an inclination for either visual, auditory, or kinesthetic *modes of communication*.[10] Although everyone has a preference for one style over another, it is likely that clients will use several sensory words and phrases during a discussion. It is important, however, for each financial planner to become attuned to listening for key terms during a client–financial planner discussion and then use similar terms when paraphrasing. Applying this approach, a financial planner will be more likely to trigger feelings of empathy, trust, and commitment among clientele. The following examples illustrate how paraphrasing can occur from a sensory-based perspective.

Visual Paraphrasing

> Planner: "What seems to be the matter today?"
>
> Client: "I am having a really hard time *focusing* on the day-to-day practicalities of tracking income and expenses. The last time we met, you asked me to *focus* in on how much I spend each day. Like I said, it is just difficult to *see* the point of tracking expenses."
>
> Planner: "You are having a hard time *seeing* how budget tracking can help you stay *focused* on your financial goals."

Auditory Paraphrasing

Client: "I keep *telling myself* that I've got to make an appointment to *talk* with an attorney about updating my will, but I always seem to *talk* myself out of it at the last minute."

Planner: "You are having a hard time *talking* yourself into making an appointment with an attorney."

Kinesthetic Paraphrasing

Planner: "So, what do you think about the idea of reallocating your portfolio to take advantage of the new tax law?

Client: "Something *smells* fishy here. I find it hard to *swallow* the notion that the government is going to do anything to *straighten out* the tax code enough to *excite* me into changing things."

Planner: "You are *feeling* skeptical about the new tax law and you kind of '*smell* a rat.'"

The third type of paraphrasing technique is referred to as a *metaphorical procedure*. By far, the metaphorical style is the most difficult to master because it requires a financial planner to hear the client's message, interpret the words, and create a paraphrase statement that does not mimic the client's words directly. Rather, a financial planner who uses this technique must quickly capture the client's meaning and restate it as either an *analogy* or *metaphor*. Phrases such as "It is an uphill fight," "This is going to be smooth sailing," and "You are not in the army anymore" are examples of metaphorical statements. Consider the following example:

Client: "I can't tell you how annoyed I am at myself. Last week my wife and I spent the whole day at the furniture store. We ended up buying a new living room sofa, love seat, and end tables. We signed up for the store's credit card because they promised zero percent interest the first year. I thought, for some odd reason, that the credit card also waived the delivery and setup fee."

Planner: "I hate to even ask, but what did it come to?"

Client: "Well, on top of the regular bill, the store hit us for a $275 delivery and setup fee. There is no way I would have bought

> the furniture knowing I had to pay that much, but I couldn't send it back because I didn't see the bill until everything was in the house. By then, it just didn't seem worth the fight."
>
> Planner: "Well, you know what they say, "There is no such thing as a free lunch.""

SUMMARY

Nondirective communication tools, such as paraphrasing, should be employed when a financial planner's objective, during a client–financial planner meeting, is to convey empathy and understanding to a client. The use of clarification, summarization, reflection, and paraphrasing techniques can be particularly effective in confirming the content and intent of a client's statements, which is integral to the process of optimal communication.

CHAPTER APPLICATIONS

1. Which of the following statements is not true in relation to paraphrasing?
   a. Paraphrasing should never add new information to a client's statement
   b. Financial planners should use paraphrasing to repeat back to a client the client's own words
   c. Financial planners should keep their paraphrasing short
   d. Paraphrasing should not be used to reflect a client's feelings
2. Which of the following terms describes the process of verifying what a client has said?
   a. Clarification
   b. Summarization
   c. Reflection
   d. Paraphrasing
3. During a client–financial planner meeting a client says the following: "I am here to get a handle on my financial situation." Based on this sentence, it is reasonable to assume that the client's sensory preference is:
   a. Auditory
   b. Visual
   c. Kinesthetic
   d. Simple

4. The use of a paraphrasing statement such as, "You may be making a mountain out of a molehill" is an example of what type of paraphrasing style?
   a. Simple
   b. Sensory
   c. Metaphorical
   d. Directive

5. Which of the following emotions are associated with financial decisions?
   a. Fear
   b. Joy
   c. Distress
   d. All of the above

6. Abed was listening to his client. As a follow up, he asked, "Can you restate what you just said?" This is an example of a(n):
   a. Clarification question
   b. Summarization question
   c. Reflection question
   d. Close-ended question

7. Toward the end of a client–financial planner meeting, Nakia says the following to her client: "I want to make sure that I understand fully what you are saying. You would like to reallocate 20 percent of your portfolio into a life cycle fund at work." This is an example of a(n):
   a. Clarification statement
   b. Summarization statement
   c. Reflection statement
   d. Review statement

8. After sitting down, Haley's client made the following statement: "I am so pleased with the way my portfolio has been performing. You are a superstar. I am telling all my friends to come work with you." Haley smiled and said, "I am so glad you are happy." This is an example of a(n):
   a. Clarification statement
   b. Summarization statement
   c. Reflection statement
   d. Review statement

9. Assume a client says the following: "I just can't see the purpose of putting 8 percent of my pay into the 401(k) plan when it appears to just go down month after month." Which of the following would be the most appropriate paraphrasing technique in response to this statement?
   a. A visual paraphrase
   b. An auditory paraphrase
   c. A kinesthetic paraphrase
   d. A metaphorical paraphrase

10. A client was complaining to her financial planner when she said, "I should have really followed your advice and diversified my assets." Her financial planner responded by saying: "You know what they say, you should never put all your eggs in one basket." This is a form of a(n):
    a. Visual paraphrase
    b. Auditory paraphrase
    c. Kinesthetic paraphrase
    d. Metaphorical paraphrase

11. Match the following terms to the appropriate sensory paraphrasing technique[12]:

    a. analyze   1. Auditory
    b. clear   2. Kinesthetic
    c. exciting   3. Visual
    d. feel
    e. focus
    f. force
    g. handle
    h. hard
    i. know
    j. picture clearly
    k. see
    l. sense
    m. smells
    n. talk
    o. tell
    p. watch

12. Find a group of classmates or colleagues and jointly develop a list of terms, verbs, adjectives, and adverbs that provide a clue into the sensory communication preferences of clients. Once the list is developed, separate the concepts into auditory, kinesthetic, and visual categories.

13. Tune into a television talk show in which a host and guests engage in active discussions. During a dialog, identify the host's preferred sensory communication style. Also determine the communication preference of each guest. Does it appear the host adapts his or her questioning to match the communication preference of each guest?

NOTES

1. F. Robinson, *Principles and Procedures in Student Counseling* (New York: Harper and Brothers, 1950).
2. A presenting issue is the stated or apparent reason a client seeks the help of a professional.

3. C. E. Izard, *Human Emotions* (New York: Plenum, 1977).

4. A. Bechara and A. R. Damasio, "The Somatic Marker Hypothesis: A Neural Theory of Economic Decision," *Games and Economic Behavior* 52 (2005): 336–372.

5. J. Sommers-Flanagan and R. Sommers-Flanagan, *Clinical Interviewing*, 3rd ed. (Hoboken, NJ: John Wiley & Sons, 2003).

6. J. Sommers-Flanagan and R. Sommers-Flanagan, *Foundations of Therapeutic Interviewing* (Needham Heights, MA: Allyn & Bacon, 1993).

7. Id.

8. Sommers-Flanagan and Sommers-Flanagan, *Clinical Interviewing*.

9. Id.

10. The concept of sensory communication preferences originated in the mid-1970s with the introduction of neurolinguistic programming therapy and counseling techniques. See R. Bandler and J. Grinder, *The Structure of Magic, Volume 1: A Book about Language and Therapy* (Palo Alto, CA: Science and Behavior Books, 1975).

7

Directive Communication

Imagine a meeting between a client and a financial planner. This is, in fact, their fourth meeting. The financial planner, in this scenario, has applied nearly all of the nondirective communication techniques presented in this book over the course of the first three meetings. She has also been very attentive to her nonverbal communication cues and mixed both open- and closed-end questioning techniques when working with the client. As a result, the client feels validated and accepted. A strong bond between the client and financial planner has been developed, with the financial planner being viewed as a trusted expert and friend.

If financial planning, as a field of study and practice, fell solely within the counseling domain, these outcomes would be considered a great success. Placing clients at the center of discussions helps to ensure that clients feel free to disclose personal information and encourages additional dialog and disclosure. In the case of the client and financial planner, it is precisely the use of nondirective communication tools and techniques that led to this point in the relationship. For many counselors and psychotherapists, this is a primary hoped-for outcome associated with therapeutic interventions. The reality is, however, that financial planners are interested in helping clients move beyond increased self-knowledge and awareness. Financial planners are engaged in creating client trust and commitment *and* bringing about positive financial change in the lives of clients. Anyone who has studied the financial planning process in any significant detail would find it quite odd if, by the fourth client–financial planner meeting, the financial planner and client had yet to move toward recommendation development and presentation of at least a few strategies for implementation.

Consider a concept from the previous chapter (shown in Figure 7.1A). Much of what has been presented in this book has been focused on nondirectional communication techniques. These tools were presented as a necessary ingredient for the creation of strong client–financial planner working relationships. Nondirectional communication, by definition, is client-centered.

FIGURE 7.1 The Continuum of Communication

Stated another way, when a financial planner uses nondirectional communication approaches, he or she steps out of the way and allows the client to be on center stage.

Questions asked by a financial planner are intended to create trust, solicit additional information, and to promote future dialog. Once the relationship has been established and appropriate data has been gathered, however, it is time to shift from a primarily client-centered perspective to one that includes direct input from the financial planner. In effect, the financial planning process is not complete until the financial planner examines the client's data, develops appropriate recommendations, and outlines an implementation strategy. By definition, these steps in the planning process require the financial planning professional to take on the role of expert and direct the client toward solutions. As shown in Figure 7.1, this change in communication approach implies moving down the continuum of communication toward financial planner–centered communication. The remainder of this chapter is devoted to discussing techniques that help clients move toward *plan implementation*.

DIRECTION: THE ESSENCE OF FINANCIAL PLANNING

Although much of what has been discussed in this book stems directly from approaches used in psychotherapy, it is important to remember that financial planning is not solely a therapeutic-based discipline. Of course, financial planners do, and should, incorporate aspects of communication that help clients move from problem to solution, but the anticipated outcome associated with financial planning is broader than improving a person's psychological well-being. In the final analysis, a financial planner's job involves improving a client's financial situation. While it is absolutely true that this may encompass changing feelings and attitudes regarding the role of money in a client's life, the primary essence of financial planning is to improve financial outcomes by increasing financial stability and optimizing decision alternatives that improve the financial well-being of the client. These functions serve to maximize the probability of a client attaining their financial goals, and assumed in turn, to support the overall happiness of the client.

Prospective clients seek the help of financial planners primarily because they have a question or concern that they are unable or unwilling to resolve themselves. Interestingly, financial planners are not the first or even primary provider of help among the general population. Where do most people turn for help when they are faced with a difficult financial question, issue, or concern? The answer is both obvious and dangerous. Family and friends tend to be the first and primary source of help for nearly all consumers.[1] The upside to relying on family and friends is that the cost is typically low, at least in regard to making a cash outlay. The downside is that friends and family may not provide sound advice and guidance relative to financial decision-making.

Only about 20 percent of Americans seek the help of financial service professionals.[2] One reason this number is so low is that the thought of visiting with a financial planner is akin to going to the dentist. It is something nearly everyone agrees may be necessary and important, but it is not a task that is engaged in with glee. This is the primary reason that financial planners ought to be experts in nondirectional communication techniques. The communication tools and strategies discussed throughout this book are designed to put a prospective client at ease and to make the planning process less intimidating and more welcoming.

In the end, however, nearly all clients still need professional help to answer financial questions, problems, and concerns. At some point, the financial planner must move down the continuum of communication and provide expert advice and guidance. There are a number of communication strategies that can be used to help clients move from contemplation to action. In the final analysis, it is the implementation of financial planner–derived recommendations that has the greatest impact in changing the lives of clients. How implementation is prompted can be influenced in any number of ways. The remainder of this chapter describes some of these directive communication techniques and tools.

INTERPRETATION

Psychoanalysts were the first to employ *interpretation* as a communication technique with clients. The traditional definition of interpretation includes references to a person's unconscious or subconscious thinking. Psychotherapists use interpretation to bring deeply held beliefs to the surface. Interpretation is a broader concept within a financial planning context. Interpretation can be thought of as helping a client articulate their thoughts and feelings using financial terminology. It is quite common for clients to have questions, concerns, and even fears about their financial situation but a lack of knowledge regarding the correct terms and conditions to describe their feelings. Imagine a client who stumbles during their description of a problem:

> Client: "I just don't know what it is, but I am feeling really anxious lately."
>
> Planner: "What seems to be the trouble?"
>
> Client: "It just seems like my wife and I are going crazy spending money. If I had to guess, I think we are way overbudget on things like furniture, clothes, and even spending on day trips."
>
> Planner: "Are you worried about paying the bills or is it something else?"
>
> Client: "I don't think it is anything like paying the bills. We have the money. I just can't explain how I am feeling."

Interpretation is not possible without a relatively high degree of knowledge about a client's financial and life situation. Given the information presented here, it is really not possible to interpret the client's feelings. Any response by the financial planner would be more of a conjecture than an interpretation.

Now assume that the client and financial planner had been working together for some time. Also assume that part of the client–financial planner engagement involved having the financial planner develop a spending plan and investment policy statement for the client. If the meeting were occurring during the client's three weeks of summer vacation, it would be possible for the financial planner to interpret the client's anxiety as follows:

> Planner: "Your anxiety is totally normal."
>
> Client: "Really?"
>
> Planner: "Absolutely. What is likely happening is that your wife is usually buying things when you are at work. The past couple of weeks you've been going with her and you've been doing the purchases. What you think is a spending spree is just what is normal for your family."
>
> Client: "Are you serious?"
>
> Planner: "I went through this last year. Whenever my husband and I have extra time on our hands, it just seems like we fill it with shopping and buying things. That is just normal, especially during vacations."

> Client: "Are you saying that I should just stop worrying and go with it?"
>
> Planner: "Well, don't really go crazy with your spending, but just know that it is okay to splurge a bit. It certainly is nothing to lose sleep over."

Notice how the financial planner responded to the client. Rather than jumping into an immediate interpretation, the financial planner first validated the client's feelings. The next step was to interpret the reason prompting the client's anxiety. In all likelihood, the client and his spouse probably were spending no more than usual. It only seemed that way because the client had more time to think about what was being purchased and the cost of the purchases. As this example illustrates, interpretation can be a useful tool to move a client beyond worrying about a situation toward other more productive behavior.

VIDEO 7A

Video 7A illustrates how a client's choice set can be expanded through the use of reframing techniques. Notice also how the financial planner includes explanation tools within the reframing discussion.

REFRAMING

Nearly everyone has heard the adage that some people view a glass as half full, while others see the same glass as half empty. *Reframing* is a technique designed to help a client shift his or her perspective. With the analogy of a glass of water, it is often useful to help clients reframe from a pessimistic viewpoint (the glass half empty) to an optimistic outlook (the glass half full).

Clients who are feeling stressed, anxious, fearful, depressed, or worried tend to avoid making long-term financial plans and decisions.[3] Clients who are exhibiting these characteristics often focus on their immediate problem(s) and search intensively for solutions. This can sometimes be a counterproductive financial planning strategy. As the client focuses more intently on one topic, he or she may lose focus on what really matters within the financial plan. It is important that financial planners learn and use reframing techniques as a way to prompt positive behavior among clients, especially those clients who may be reluctant to implement recommendations.

Consider a situation in which a client holds very strong political beliefs. Over the course of a lifetime, these beliefs can begin to shade all types of financial planning decisions, often in a negative manner. The period between 2009 and 2013 marks such a period of time. In 2009, the United States was just beginning to emerge from what many have called the Great Recession. Many investors found federal policies related to health care and taxes discomforting at this time. Some of these investors pulled assets from traditional securities markets and moved to what have been called safe haven assets, such as commodities and collectibles in anticipation of social chaos and market instability. What actually occurred was a historical increase in the price of equities. A large percentage of American investors missed out on what, in retrospect, was a great bull run in the markets. Some of this missed opportunity resulted from political beliefs clouding perceptions of reality. While it is true that a progressive political agenda was in full force in Washington, DC, it is also true that the Federal Reserve was increasing the money supply at astronomical and unprecedented rates. This fact, for those who focused on the fundamentals shaping the market, superseded the role of politics in creating the direction for future stock prices. Financial planners who were able to reframe their clients' disappointment in social policies (at least among those who were worried about these issues) toward a realization that the Federal Reserve was supporting the markets were in a position to capture higher returns. Here is how one discussion might have played out:

Client: "I cannot believe that the outcome of the election. What were the American people thinking?"

Planner: "It was certainly an interesting election."

Client: "I just cannot see any positives coming from the election. The health care law is going to balloon the deficit, and the politicians are going to raise taxes on everyone. How can anything good come from this?"

Planner: "That is definitely one way to look at it."

Client: "You cannot be suggesting that there is anything good in all of this . . .?"

Planner: "Let's look at this from a different angle. Don't you think folks at the Federal Reserve are worried about the economy?"

Client: "I have no idea. We've got high unemployment, no growth, and rising taxes. Nothing good can come from this."

Planner: "Ah, but that may be exactly why there is opportunity here. The Federal Reserve is going to continue to promote quantitative easing."

Client: "What is that?"

> Planner: "Just a fancy name for increasing the money supply by buying bonds, and I mean a lot of bonds. Interest rates are going to go way down."
>
> Client: "Are you saying that is a good thing?"
>
> Planner: "You bet. When interest rates fall, it makes stocks a lot more attractive. Also, companies can continue to cut costs with little downside risk. This could be one of the best times in our lives to be buying stock."
>
> Client: "So, you are saying that we can let the politicians make money for us."
>
> Planner: "Well, maybe not that exactly, but I am okay letting the politicians gripe and moan about things. Let's stay focused on the fundamentals. As long as interest rates are falling, we are in good—no great—shape."

The manner in which the financial planner reframed the client's perspective was not confrontational or adversarial. It would be, in fact, nearly impossible to know the political affiliation of the financial planner. Even in cases in which a reframing technique does not result in an altered behavior, reframing can be an effective tool in creating additional dialog, as well as planting a seed of behavioral change for the future.

EXPLANATION

The great equalizer among people who are faced with complex decisions is information. While interpretation and reframing are valuable directive communication tools, explanation may be a financial planner's best, and most widely used, technique for leading clients to behavioral change. Sommers-Flanagan and Sommers-Flanagan[4] defined an *explanation* as "a descriptive statement used to make something plain or understandable" (p. 91).

As shown in Figure 7.2, the types of questions asked by clients often change based on the stage of the financial planning process. Clients are likely to ask one of three questions that require explanation at the outset of a client–financial planner engagement. During the early stages of the financial planning process, clients will have questions about the process itself, including costs, time lines, obligations, and expectations. At this stage of the process, client questions will likely change to definitional clarifications. Although it seems basic to those working in the profession, few prospective clients truly know the difference between, say, a mutual fund and an

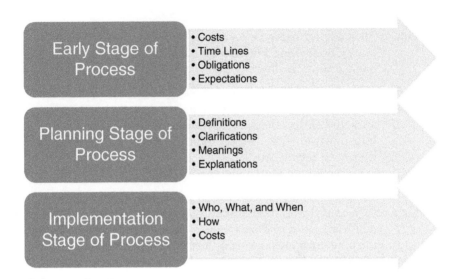

FIGURE 7.2   Types of Client Questions Mapped to Stages in the Planning Process

exchange traded fund or whole and universal life insurance. Rather than keep clients guessing or referring to the Internet for guidance, financial planners need to provide detailed explanations to keep clients moving toward plan implementation. During the actual implementation stage of the planning process, client questions will become more practical. For example, explanations for "who, what, when, how, and how much" related to plan implementation need to be provided.

Examples and counterexamples of effective explanations can be found in daily activities. One of cable television's most popular shows, for example, involves a cast of eccentric individuals who travel from town to town bidding on storage lockers. Toward the end of every show, each winning bidder takes one item to a specialist to obtain a price quote. In nearly every episode, the winning bidders feign interest in the expert's descriptions by appearing to listen attentively to the expert. While being polite, the storage locker bidders are interested in one thing: the price of the item if they sold it.

VIDEO 7B

Video 7B demonstrates how a financial planner both correctly and incorrectly provides explanations. In one case, the planner provides an explanation that although makes the planner sound knowledgeable, likely has an adverse effect on the client–financial planner working

> alliance. In the other case, notice how the planner provides an expla-
> nation that not only increases the knowledge of the client but also
> strengthens trust and rapport.

Fortunately, individuals and families that seek the help of financial planners are not storage locker bidders. Rather than profess interest in a financial planner's explanations, nearly all clients need and want descriptions
and clarifications of the planning process, financial products, and expected
outcomes. Financial planners who provide ongoing explanations about
products, services, and research tend to create a social bond with clients.
Carefully crafted explanations build *social capital*. The appropriate use
of explanations can help financial planners build an ongoing expectation
among clients that asking questions is not only appropriate but also expected.
Here is an example of how a financial planner might explain the basic data-
gathering stage of the financial planning process:

Planner: "I know that you have lots of questions about our firm, our
services, and financial planning in general. Is there anything
that comes to mind immediately that is unclear?"

Client: "I am not really sure what to even ask."

Planner: "That is totally understandable. Why don't we start with
what we did today and hopefully will do over the next couple
of weeks? Does that sound okay?"

Client: "Sure."

Planner: "Our process is very transparent. When you leave
today, Andy, my para-planner, will give you a packet
of information that you need to fill out and bring back
next week. When we get together, Andy will take your
information and put it into our system. We will then start
identifying financial planning goals and objectives. By the
third meeting, we will have some preliminary reports for
you to review. How does that sound?"

Client: "Okay, but when you say a report, what does that mean?"

Planner: "Great question. The initial reports will give us a picture of
what you are currently earning and spending on a yearly
basis. We call that a cash-flow statement. We will also

(continued)

> (*Continued*)
>
> calculate your net worth, which simply involves taking all of your assets, or a total value of what you own, and subtracting out your debts, for a total value of what you own. We will also have some other documentation to share at that time."
>
> Client: "Okay, that makes sense. I have always wanted to know my net worth. Sounds kind of fun."

Clients often need just an explanation as a form of reassurance. Consider a prospective client who recently inherited $300,000. In this situation, it is important to understand that this amount of inheritance is likely a sizable sum for the prospective client. He naturally assumes that the complexities associated with investing such a large dollar amount must be incredibly difficult. Furthermore, he is unsure whether the financial planner sitting across the table has the skills and ability to deal with his concerns. Explanation can be an ideal technique to lead the client toward engagement. Here is a snippet from their conversation:

> Client: "This is a relatively large sum of money. Probably more than I will ever see in my life again."
>
> Planner: "It is important for you to make sure that your inheritance is invested wisely."
>
> Client: "That is my point exactly."
>
> Planner: "Your concern is the same as every one of our clients. It really does not matter if they just received $10,000 or $1,000,000. They want to know that the money will be invested appropriately."
>
> Client: "Do you have other clients with this kind of nest egg?"
>
> Planner: "Absolutely. Our firm's typical client has about $500,000 under management. It is not uncommon for some clients to receive inheritances of more than $1,000,000."
>
> Client: "That kind of makes me a small fish then."
>
> Planner: "No, not at all. Remember, those $500,000 accounts had to start somewhere. We construct portfolios for clients that are based on each person's unique time horizon, risk tolerance, and objectives. Nothing we've talked about today causes me any concern in terms of an investment policy for you."
>
> Client: "That makes me feel a lot better."

This example illustrates how an explanation focused on providing clients with information about their situation, and how it is similar to or different from others, can create client comfort and promote client action. Rather than being concerned about the financial planner's ability to handle the inheritance, the explanation provided a framework of confidence that the financial planner has dealt with much larger issues successfully.

ADVICE

One of the most financial planner–centered forms of directive communication is *advice*. In its simplest form, advice involves giving a client direction about what to do in a particular situation. When clients do reach out to a financial planner, they are seeking advice regarding ways to improve their situation. This insight, from a financial planning perspective, has both a negative and positive side. As discussed in previous chapters, financial planners tend to be action oriented and solution focused. There is sometimes a temptation to move too quickly from client engagement to problem analysis and solution presentation. This temptation to jump ahead is almost always signaled from the client. After all, most clients appear to be asking for specific advice. However, a financial planner who moves too quickly from nondirective communication to providing advice can sabotage the planning process.

VIDEO 7C

Video 7C demonstrates how a financial planner both correctly and incorrectly provides advice. In one case, the planner provides advice before seeking to fully understand the client and associated contextual factors (that is, not enough nondirective communication). Notice whether the client discounts the advice in the first scenario as compared to the second.

Clients who present an issue and then soon after receive advice from a financial planner may discount the counsel. Why? The *discounting of advice* occurs primarily because even though clients typically ask for prescriptions, much of the counseling literature suggests that clients really want problem exploration. Advice given too quickly may be discounted. Consider a situation in which a prospective client visits a life insurance agent. The client begins to discuss education-funding wishes for a grandchild. During the brief conversation, imagine that the agent leans back in her chair and says something like, "The advice I give everyone in your situation is to purchase universal life insurance." This advice may be perfectly valid. The client may interpret the solution, however, as premature and tied too closely to the agent's occupational choice.

A key takeaway is this: before providing advice, it is important to explore what other solutions have already been considered or tried in the past. The life insurance agent, in the example just noted, moved too quickly in providing her advice. Had she employed other communication tools and techniques, she might have learned that the client once had a universal life insurance policy that lapsed because of returns falling below projections. The prospective client may be not only reluctant to use this type of product, he may actually be opposed to the idea. The agent, by jumping to the advice stage of communication, will have missed an opportunity to learn more about her client. She also will miss a sales opportunity.

Providing advice has a positive side as well. Assuming that a financial planner has taken the time to learn what other strategies and ideas have been used to solve a client's question or concern, and that the opportunity has been thoroughly outlined, providing advice shines the spotlight directly on the financial planner's unique skills and talents. Advice, when placed in this light, turns a financial planner from being merely an adviser to an expert. The following example illustrates how a financial planner can use directive communication tools as a way to provide advice:

Client: "I have been struggling with a big financial question for a while."

Planner: "Let's talk about it."

Client: "My son has just been accepted to a local university. That is the good news. The bad news is that tuition and other fees come to over $60,000 per year."

Planner: "Ouch."

Client: "I know that we've been saving all along in the 529 plan, but even after grants and other help from the university, there is no way that we can cover the tuition expense. What do you think I should do?"

Planner: "Before jumping into solutions, let's talk about a few things."

Client: "Okay."

Planner: "Have you been talking to anyone else about this problem?"

Client: "Yes."

Planner: "Tell me a bit about who you've been talking with and what they've recommended."

Client: "My wife and I met with the financial aid folks at the university. Their advice was to take out loans to cover the tuition."

Planner: "How did that make you feel?"

Client: "Not so good. As I figure it, I'd be in debt until my retirement. Now, I love my son, but that is a lot of money."

Planner: "Is there anyone else you've talked to about this?"

Client: "I hate to say it, but I've been talking with my brother-in-law. His son just graduated from college. He had some of the same funding issues."

Planner: "What did he recommend?"

Client: "He said I should take a distribution from my 401(k) plan."

Planner: "What was his reasoning?"

Client: "As I recall, he said something like the distribution could be taken penalty-free because I would be using it for college tuition."

Planner: "What do you think of that recommendation?"

Client: "I am leaning toward that direction. It makes sense in that I can access the money. I won't pay a tax penalty, and I will not be in debt for the rest of my working life."

Planner: "What other advice have your received?"

Client: "That is basically it."

Planner: "Those are certainly doable options, but I have another idea that might appeal to you."

Client: "Well, that's what I am here for."

Planner: "Great. Let me start by saying that I don't like the idea of using tax-inefficient debt unless you have to do it."

Client: "What do you mean by 'tax-inefficient?'"

Planner: "Given your household income, if you take out a parent loan for your son, you are not going to receive a tax benefit on the interest paid. So, I would not do the local university loan package at this point."

Client: "So, I should take a distribution from the retirement account?"

(continued)

(*Continued*)

Planner: "Not exactly. Did you know that your 401(k) plan has a loan provision?"

Client: "I remember something like that, but I was told plan loans are dangerous."

Planner: "Plan loans can be dangerous, but in your case, this may be the best way for you to help your son through college. Rather than take a parent loan, you simply borrow the money from yourself. You will pay interest on the loan, but the majority of the interest will be credited back to your account. That way, you can help your son and not wipe out your retirement savings. If, on the other hand, you take your brother-in-law's advice, you will end up paying taxes on the full distribution amount."

Client: "Well, he did not tell me about paying taxes. I just assumed no penalty meant no taxation at all."

Planner: "In this situation, your brother-in-law probably didn't know all of the tax implications of his advice."

Although this example is oversimplified, it does illustrate how a financial planner could obtain information from a client before prescribing a strategic recommendation. Obviously, details associated with recommendation formation and implementation will follow, but as an initial conversation, this advice-giving procedure allows a financial planner to differentiate his or her advice from others in a way that adds credibility to the information provided.

SUGGESTION

The terms *suggest* and *advise* are often used interchangeably. Sommers-Flanagan and Sommers-Flanagan,[5] in their text on clinical interviewing for counselors, noted that while these terms are sometimes confused, they are distinct concepts within an adviser's directive communication toolbox. Whereas advising involves giving direction to a client, the act of suggesting involves helping a client choose a course of action using his or her own initiative. Financial planners tend to be most comfortable providing advice. Advice, when compared to suggestion, is easier, simpler, and more direct. Suggestion, on the other hand, tends to be milder and less direct.

Nearly all financial planners and other financial service professionals identify more closely with either models of advice or suggestion. The preference toward one or the other is driven, in large part, by the academic training and background of the professional. Financial planners whose background is grounded in pure financial planning, economics, finance, or a related business field often have a tendency to fall back on providing *direct advice* when working with clients. This is another way of saying that their theoretical orientation is *advice-based*. Those working in the field whose training was obtained in the social sciences may exhibit a preference for suggestion. Their theoretical orientation is likely to be *information-based*. Psychologists, counselors, and psychotherapists tend to be less inclined to provide direct advice to their clients. They prefer instead to bring together multiple solutions, present the advantages and disadvantages, and then allow the client to choose among the alternatives. Here is how a financial planner who prefers suggestion might go about addressing a client's education funding question:

Client: "I have been struggling with a big financial question for a while."

Planner: "Let's talk about it."

Client: "My son has just been accepted to a local university. That is the good news. The bad news is that tuition and other fees come to over $60,000 per year."

Planner: "Ouch."

Client: "I know that we've been saving all along in the 529 plan, but even after grants and other help from the university, there is no way that we can cover the tuition expense. What do you think I should do?"

Planner: "There are a number of possible solutions. Let's talk about some of them."

Client: "Okay."

Planner: "First, have you been talking to anyone else about this problem?"

Client: "Yes."

Planner: "Tell me a bit about who you've been talking with and what they've recommended."

Client: "My wife and I met with the financial aid folks at the university. Their advice was to take out loans to cover the tuition."

(continued)

(*Continued*)

Planner: "Is there anyone else you've talked to about this?"

Client: "I hate to say it, but I've been talking with my brother-in-law. His son just graduated from Vanderbilt. He had some of the same funding issues."

Planner: "What did he recommend?"

Client: "He said I should take a distribution from my 401(k) plan."

Planner: "Are there any other ideas that have come to mind?"

Client: "Not really. That is the reason I am here. What do you think I should do?"

Planner: "Well, the two strategies you already have seem reasonable enough. You can take out a loan or you can take a distribution from your retirement account. There are a couple of other ideas that we should throw into the mix as well."

Client: "What do you mean?"

Planner: "Did you know that your 401(k) plan has a loan provision?"

Client: "I remember something like that, but I was told plan loans are dangerous."

Planner: "Plan loans can be dangerous but not always. If you go this direction, you simply borrow the money from yourself. You will pay interest on the loan, but the majority of the interest will be credited back to your account."

Client: "That sounds interesting."

Planner: "Another alternative is to explore lower-cost colleges and universities."

Client: "But my son is really intent on attending the local university. What do you think I should do?"

Planner: "My suggestion is to talk to your wife and son about what they really want to do. If the local university truly is the school for your son, then you are going to need to use some of your family assets one way or another. While we can optimize a solution, what it really comes down to is your comfort level. You may find that the cost of the local university education is too high, in which case the fourth alternative may be something to consider."

It should be obvious that the financial planner, in this case, prefers the fourth lower-cost solution but is reluctant to advise against the local university education. This reluctance may stem from the financial planner's knowledge of the client's temperament and decision-making approach. The hesitancy may also stem directly from the financial planner's theoretical orientation. In other words, the financial planner may feel that it is inappropriate to give a client direct advice regarding a situation. Some financial planners, in fact, believe that their primary duty to a client is to bring together several plausible and sensible solutions to any question. Within this framework of financial planning, it is up to the client to choose from the available strategies. Of course, the financial planner will help implement the choice, but in the final analysis, the client is responsible for strategy selection.

While the use of suggestion, as a mild form of directive communication, is used extensively by some financial planners, financial therapists, and financial counselors, this technique does have a significant downside associated with its use. Specifically, clients can get easily confused. Unlike therapeutic situations in which a client may intuitively or unconsciously know which course of action is best for his or her situation, this is often times not the case when a client faces a financial decision. Simply providing a client with reasonable alternatives may not be viewed as a value-added service among consumers. More often than not, clients seek the help of a financial planner to obtain the best and most beneficial recommendation. While clients may be interested in alternatives, they do expect, in most situations, to receive an *optimized recommendation*. The communication of the best-fit recommendation is often better received when given as advice rather than through suggestion. Saying this, however, it is still important for financial planners to understand when suggestion may be appropriate. For example, the technique is particularly useful when a client must decide between choices in which no clear optimal solution is present.[6]

URGING

Urging a client to take immediate action is an important, but less used, form of directive communication. Urging tends to be crisis-driven. As such, this communication technique should rarely be used when working directly with clients. This is not to say, however, that urging is rarely used in practice. A large percentage of financial planners who are in practice today are sometimes forced to plead and urge clients to take action on a daily basis. Lack of implementation, after all, is one of the largest obstacles facing financial planners and their clientele.

VIDEO 7D

Video 7D shows how urging a client to take action does not need to be confrontational or provocative. In this example, notice how the financial planner urges the client to action by providing a definite time line of implementation.

The communication literature suggests that financial planners and counselors who find themselves urging clients to action on a regular basis have not fully learned and adopted the key nondirective communication tools presented earlier in this book. It is precisely the lack of a strong client–financial planner relationship that most often leads to lack of implementation issues. Because the bonds of communication are weak, the trust needed on the part of the client in his or her financial planner may also be fragile.

Urging, as a tool within the directive communication toolbox, comes into play when a client faces a dramatic crisis. Urging should come packaged as simple and direct advice. Here is an example:

Client: "I received a letter from the IRS yesterday."

Planner: "That is never a good sign. What did the letter say?"

Client: "My husband and I are being audited."

Planner: "What's the time line for the audit?

Client: "We have an appointment in two weeks."

Planner: "Is there anything you need from our office?"

Client: "I am not sure. I was hoping that you could help us."

Planner: "Certainly, I am going to help. I do need to let you know right up front that you should not represent yourself during the audit. Who has been doing your taxes?"

Client: "My husband has a friend who does taxes on the side. He's been filing our taxes the past few years."

Planner: "Is this guy a CPA or enrolled agent?"

Client: "No. He just works part time for one of the big tax return firms during tax season."

Planner: "Okay. Here is what you need to do. And this is urgent. You need to get in touch with an enrolled agent today or tomorrow. I've got a colleague who does nothing but tax

> representation. You need to see him, or someone who does similar work, as soon as possible."
>
> Client: "Is it really that big of a deal? I was figuring just going down to see what the issue was all about."
>
> Planner: "I cannot urge you enough to get the help of an enrolled agent. They can represent you before the IRS and probably resolve all the issues quickly and with as little disturbance to your life as possible."

Financial planners who constantly urge and plead with clients to take action reduce their effectiveness in persuading clients toward action. As illustrated with this example, when urging is used judiciously and with care, clients will know that action is of paramount importance. Other situations in which urging may be required include issues related to divorce, separation, natural disasters, casualty and theft losses, bankruptcy, foreclosure, and other topics about which strict time limits come into play.

CONFRONTATION

Clients sometimes have an inaccurate perception of the client–financial planner relationship, the financial planning process, or the marketplace in which decisions are made. Occasionally, clients will hold incongruent views that negatively affect their financial future. In these rare and limited circumstances, it may be appropriate for a financial planner to confront a client in an effort to alter the client's attitudes and behaviors.

Confrontation involves voicing a disagreement. The act of confrontation does not need to be violent, shameful, or hurtful. Confrontation, however, should be direct and forceful. Before venturing forward, it is important to note that the use of confrontation should be minimized and avoided except in rare situations. Confrontation, by its very nature, can destroy much of the bonding between client and financial planner that occurs throughout the planning process. As such, this communication technique ought to be used only in cases in which a financial planner knows that the emotional tendencies of the client are amenable to conflict and when the financial planner has evidence to support the confrontation.

Before providing an example, it is worth mentioning again that this communication tool is a high-risk option, but it is important to include here because, although rarely used in practice, the technique can prompt an otherwise complacent client into taking action. Keep in mind that one of three outcomes can follow a direct confrontation: the client will (1) deny the validity of the disagreement, (2) accept the critique, or (3) partially admit to being wrong. Two of the three outcomes will likely result in the client terminating the financial planning engagement or altering his or her judgment of the financial planner's abilities. Given the potential negative impact a confrontation can have on the client–financial planner relationship, some communication experts recommend that this technique is used only as a last resort.

The following is an example of confrontation used by a financial planner who has been working with a client who is going through a mid-life crisis:

Client: "Thanks again for seeing me on such short notice."

Planner: "Not a problem at all. What is on your mind?"

Client: "I need to withdraw $65,000 from my IRA."

Planner: "Really? Why the sudden need for so much cash?"

Client: "Based on our last conversation, I am kind of reluctant to tell you."

Planner: "You don't need to tell me. I just want to remind you that this will be third withdrawal this month from the account."

Client: "Yeah, I know, but I need the money. I am going to buy a new car, and I'd rather just pay cash than take out a loan. Anyway, the returns on the IRA have been so bad that it doesn't really matter."

Planner: "Well, one of the reasons the returns have not been so great is that I have had to reallocate the portfolio by moving the account balance into cash just to cover these withdrawals."

Client: "So what? It is my money."

Planner: "Absolutely, the money in the account is yours and you are free to do what you like with the assets. Let me just lay this out for you. Over the past few months, you have withdrawn about one-third of your IRA account value. I told you the last time that these distributions are going to throw you into a higher marginal tax bracket next year. Plus, you will end up paying penalties on everything you've taken out. Going down this route is really imprudent. You are basically destroying your retirement plan, and for what? A new car? I've got to tell you, that it is an unwise decision."

> Client: "What is unwise? Buying the car or taking the distribution?"
>
> Planner: "Both. I do not want to lose you as a client, but I also don't want you to keep making these types of decisions that will ultimately screw up your financial future. You need to really think about this purchase and determine if you want to go forward with the distribution. If you say 'yes,' then we will have to figure out our next steps."

Note how the financial planner confronts without giving an ultimatum. Although it is implied that the financial planner may terminate the relationship in the future, she has not yet stepped across that invisible communication boundary line from confrontation to ultimatum.

ULTIMATUM

Sometimes, a financial planner must move from urging a client toward action, to confrontation, and finally to the stage of *ultimatum*. If confrontation presented the potential to sabotage the client–financial planner relationship, an ultimatum could be seen as the grenade of communication—it is likely to generate as much chaos as it solves. Ultimatums occur when a client's behavior becomes dysfunctional and disruptive to a financial planner's practice.

There is an old maxim among financial planners related to the Pareto principle that 20 percent of clients generate 80 percent of a firm's revenue, and that 80 percent of a firm's problems are caused by 20 percent of clients. Some financial planning consultants recommend that financial planners terminate clients on a yearly basis as a way to improve practice efficiency through the reduction of problem clients and low-revenue clientele. The factors involved in culling clients from a practice are beyond the scope of this book, but if this is an approach that is chosen, it is likely that a financial planner will need to provide some clients with an ultimatum. Here is an example:

> Planner: "Thanks for coming in today. The reason I've asked you for a visit is because my team members and I have been reviewing your file. Did you know that over the past three years you have implemented only two of our firm's recommendations?"
>
> Client: "Really, I had no idea."
>
> *(continued)*

(*Continued*)

Planner: "We see this as a problem. First, you are paying us a relatively high fee for planning services, which is really a waste of your money at this point. Second, and maybe more importantly, we have a long waiting list of prospective clients. While it may sound odd, we really are not interested in billing clients when we are not providing service. We would much prefer to have a new client who is actively engaged in the financial planning process than someone who is less interested in implementing our recommendations."

Client: "Are you firing me?"

Planner: "I would not say that. I simply want you to think about the value of our services compared to the price you have been paying. Let me put it this way. I simply cannot continue to bill you unless there is increased engagement on your part. How about we meet again in two weeks to talk about our future together?"

In a sense, this example combines both confrontation and an ultimatum. The financial planner has pointed out that the client is underusing the firm's services. The financial planner has also noted that others would love to be a client of the firm. It is at this point that the ultimatum appears.

The use of ultimatums is extremely rare in financial planning practice. Issues related to *ethics* and *standards of conduct* sometimes trigger this extreme communication technique. Imagine a situation in which a financial planner is asked by his client to open a joint brokerage account in the client's name with a stranger of the opposite sex. Picture as well that the financial planner knows the client's wife and children, although they are not part of his clientele. It is apparent, at least from all indications, that the client may be having an extramarital affair. Federal, state, and firm rules dictate rules regarding disclosure of personal information to third parties. In this situation, it would be unethical (and possibly illegal) for the financial planner to disclose the new account information to the client's spouse. It is possible, however, that the financial planner might find the situation to be morally incorrect. This is the type of situation in which the financial planner may wish to give the client an ultimatum regarding the client–financial planner relationship. In this case, it is likely that the financial planner will lose the client, but at least the financial planner will have removed an ethical dilemma from her working relationships.

SUMMARY

Much of what has been discussed in previous chapters was presented as tools or techniques for use in establishing and enhancing the client–financial planner relationship. Nondirective communication techniques were shown to be primarily client-centered. Placing the client at the forefront of nondirectional communication is an ideal procedure that enhances client dialog, comfort, and sharing.

At some point in every financial planning scenario, the direction of communication must move from being primarily client-centered to emphasizing the role of the financial planner. This chapter has described some of the most widely used communication tools and techniques used to direct clients toward action and plan implementation. The least direct techniques include interpretation, reframing, and suggestion. These tools can be used to help a client begin to arrive at decision points when faced with planning choices. Explanation and advice were shown to be the most widely used directive communication techniques used in practice. Not only does explanation, for example, serve to bring greater understanding of complex issues, this communication technique often cements bonds of trust between client and financial planner by illustrating the financial planner's expertise. The chapter concluded with a review of three methods of directive communication that should be used with caution and great care. Urging, confrontation, and ultimatums can all be effective in cajoling a client into a decision and action. These communication practices, however, can also cause strain within the client–financial planner working alliance.

CHAPTER APPLICATIONS

1. The primary purpose of financial planning is to
   a. Help clients come to grips with their feelings and attitudes about money
   b. Improve the financial outcomes experienced by a client
   c. Provide direct advice about financial questions and problems
   d. Allow financial planners to illustrate their expertise within the financial planning process

2. Helping a client shift his or her perspective regarding a financial issue involves which type of directive communication technique?
   a. Interpretation
   b. Reframing
   c. Explaining
   d. Urging

3. There is a form of communication that places a client in a position of choosing a course of action based on his or her own initiative. This is known as
   a. Suggestion
   b. Advice
   c. Reframing
   d. Ultimatum

4. Imagine a situation in which a financial planner says something like: "You need to make a quick decision. The markets close in 20 minutes, and you must take action to liquidate your position." This is closest to what type of directive communication technique?
   a. Ultimatum
   b. Confrontation
   c. Urging
   d. Explanation

5. A financial planner whose preference was to provide clients with several suitable recommendations from which to choose when making a financial planning decision would be said to hold
   a. An advice-based theoretical orientation
   b. A generalist theoretical orientation
   c. An information-based theoretical orientation
   d. A quantitative theoretical orientation

6. During a client–financial planner discussion, the clients says, "I am really nervous the markets are going to fall. I am losing sleep worrying about the markets." After a brief pause, the financial planner says, "I am also worried about the markets, at least in the short run. I have given it a lot of thought. There is no need for you to lose any sleep." The financial planner's response is a type of:
   a. Interpretation
   b. Reframing
   c. Explaining
   d. Urging

7. A client called her financial planner in a panic. She said that she had just come from her payroll office and was told she had to make a retirement plan choice that day. She also said that she didn't understand the difference between the company stock and the mutual funds offered. In response, the financial planner said the following: "Lots of people get confused about stocks and mutual funds. Essentially, if you purchase the stock you are buying directly into your company. If you buy one of the mutual funds, you are purchasing an investment that is not directly tied to your company. Some might say that the mutual fund is safer because the fund owns shares in many different companies." This response is closest to be a(n):
   a. Interpretation
   b. Framing
   c. Explanation
   d. Urging

8. It is late in the day and a financial adviser is yelling into the phone saying: "Tom, the markets are falling. You must sell those shares right now. You don't have a choice. If you do not sell, I am not sure what I can do for you." This is an example of what type of communication technique?
   a. Interpretation
   b. Framing
   c. Explanation
   d. Urging
9. Which of the following communication techniques is most likely to result in a client–financial planner relationship termination?
   a. Urging
   b. Confrontation
   c. Ultimatum
   d. Paraphrase
10. Marcel is most interested in creating a client–financial planner relationship based on trust and commitment. Given his objective, which of the following communication techniques promotes this goal?
    a. Explanation
    b. Framing
    c. Urging
    d. Confrontation
11. Ask a friend, classmate, or colleague to practice a directive communication technique with you. Invite the person to think of a situation in which he or she would have liked or currently need advice. Using both open- and closed-end questioning techniques, obtain as much information as possible about the problem, past actions to solve the problem, and outcomes associated with past actions. After this information has been obtained, attempt to provide an interpretation of the situation.
12. Work with one or more classmates or colleagues and develop a list of commonly held cause and effect relationships in the financial planning field. For example, some people believe that holding precious metals is an effective hedge against inflation, and as such, they argue that if inflation increases, gold prices ought to increase as well. Once the list has been developed, formulate a counterargument that illustrates how each relationship can be reframed from a financial planning perspective.

NOTES

1. J. E. Grable and S.-H. Joo, "A Further Examination of Financial Help-Seeking Behavior," *Journal of Financial Counseling and Planning* 12, no. 1 (2001): 55–73.
2. GAO, "Report to Congressional Addressees: Consumer Finance," www.gao .gov/new.items/d11235.pdf.

3. A. Bechara and A. R. Damasio, "The Somatic Marker Hypothesis: A Neural Theory of Economic Decision," *Games and Economic Behavior* 52 (2005): 336–372.

4. J. Sommers-Flanagan and R. Sommers-Flanagan, *Clinical Interviewing*, 3rd ed. (Hoboken, NJ: John Wiley & Sons, 2003).

5. Id.

6. This is called a Hobson's choice in the economic literature.

8

Trust, Culture, and Communication Taboos

The dual concepts of client trust and commitment have been presented and described widely throughout this book. Nearly every communication tool and technique described herein is something that a financial planner can use to improve the client–financial planner relationship and enhance client trust and commitment. The purpose of this chapter is to provide a clear definition of what trust means, as well as describe the primary ways a financial planner can establish trust with clients. Of foremost importance is the issue of cultural influence on both communication processes and the formation of trust. As is described in this chapter, many of the daily verbal and nonverbal communication approaches used by some financial planners can be interpreted as culturally inappropriate and sometimes offensive. No one wants to discredit his or her work and destroy client trust, but this may be happening inadvertently. Financial planners who have a solid understanding of the interaction between cultural values and norms and communication strategies will be in a much better position when it comes to creating, maintaining, and growing his or her financial planning practice.

As authors and university professors, one of the greatest joys associated with writing and teaching about financial planning involves our ongoing involvement with financial planning professionals. Although some firms attempt to create a mold of what they perceive to be a proxy for success, the fact is that financial planners come in all types of shapes, sizes, and colors. This is true both literally and metaphorically. We have run into very successful financial planners who some would describe as boisterous and overbearing. Other very prosperous advisers are meek and timid. Some wear flashy clothes and drive fast cars. Others wear suits from discount stores and drive pickup trucks. More than once we have had a financial planner give a guest lecture only to have students after class ask, "Who would ever work with that jerk?" Our answer is almost always, "There are a lot of people who do, and there are even more who would like to."

One of the secrets underlying the practice of financial planning, and most other professional activities in which clients work with a well-educated professional, is that what really matters is how clients perceive the trustworthiness of their financial planner. The level of client trust in his or her adviser is linked directly with the probability of recommendation implementation. Nearly all of the literature that describes the processes involved in trust development point to one fact: clients who perceive their financial planner as similar to who they are personally almost always rate their financial planner highly in terms of competence and ultimately trustworthiness.[1] This, in turn, leads to implementation of recommendations. Clients, like all people, have cultural preferences. *Culture,* according to Kreuter and McClure,[2] includes the values, beliefs, practices, norms, roles, social regularities, and styles of communication that are learned and shared generationally. This is the reason a flamboyant and self-assured financial planner can simultaneously attract some high net worth clients while repelling other clients. If this type of financial planner can find enough like-minded clients who share his or her cultural preferences, then the adviser is one step closer to success.

The opposite is also true. Financial planners who fail to account for the cultural preferences of their clientele are likely to fail in the profession. If a financial planner's personal communication style does not match the cultural profile and preferences of potential clients, the odds of success, sadly, for that financial planner are very low.

UNDERSTANDING A CLIENT'S CULTURAL ATTRIBUTES

Interpersonal communication and culture interact at three individual preference levels[3]: (1) responsibility preferences, (2) interpersonal preferences, and (3) risk management preferences. *Responsibility preferences* refer to the way in which someone views his or her relationship with others. Think about a continuum with two extremes, as shown in Figure 8.1. On one end is someone whose cultural socialization represents *individualism*. This is sometimes called an *independent norm*. On the other end are those whose culture supports *collectivism*. This end of the spectrum is sometimes referred to as an *interdependent norm*.

Consider the typical child who is raised in an American home. The general American cultural norm involves the encouragement of independent thinking, acting, and living. Uniqueness is valued within individualistic cultures. While Americans often assume that people around them, both those

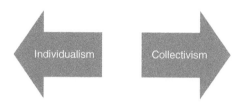

FIGURE 8.1   Continuum of Responsibility Preferences

living in the United States and around the world, share a cultural perspective that values individualistic action, the reality is quite different. The majority of people living today hold a cultural perspective that lies closer to the collectivism preference on the continuum. While the term *collectivism* is sometimes associated with socialism, within communication theory the term should be thought of as *interdependence*.[4] A child raised within a collectivist culture will tend to value conformity, concern for others, and inclusiveness.

Fortunately, there are communication clues that can provide a hint as to a person's cultural responsibility preference. A client who uses "I" and "you" frequently, compared to "we" or "us," probably holds an independent *cultural perspective*. Using this simple form of evaluation can be the difference between cementing a client relationship and losing a client. Within most interdependent cultures, children are raised to value family relationships. This means that there is an implicit assumption that younger family members will help their older immediate and extended family in times of personal and financial stress. These obligations can sometimes conflict with recommendations made in the financial planning process. Someone who holds a strong interpersonal cultural preference will be willing to sacrifice his or her savings and personal goals to support others in their family and community. It is easy to imagine conflict arising within the client–financial planner relationship, especially if the client's financial planner holds an individualistic cultural norm.

INTERPERSONAL PREFERENCE

Interpersonal preferences are the second area in which culture and communication interact. An *interpersonal preference* refers to the way in which someone expects social interactions to occur. Issues related to formality, status, power, and structure are all shaped by a person's cultural socialization. As shown in Figure 8.2, interpersonal cultural preferences can be grouped as being primarily "low power/distance" or "high power/distance."[5]

FIGURE 8.2 Classification Based on Interpersonal Cultural Preference

Imagine, for a moment, the typical boutique-size financial planning firm operating in the United States. Typically, this type of firm is owned and managed by one or two principals. While staff have particular jobs and responsibilities, the office environment tends to be one in which the owners and staff work informally, using polite requests. Managers in these firms typically expect their staff to provide honest feedback and opinions. While the management team holds ultimate decision-making power, there is usually an implied sharing of decision making among the staff. On any particular day, it would not be surprising to find one of the owners involved in mundane tasks like cleaning a client conference room, working alongside a staff member in the development of a specialized spreadsheet, or answering routine phone calls while a staff member is out of the office. This firm's interpersonal culture is based on *low power/distance* relationships.

Now contrast this with a financial planning firm operating in a major Asian city. In this firm, each staff member's roles and obligations are explicitly known and communicated. Personal roles and obligations are also strictly enforced. Within such a firm, differences in power are extreme. Formality rules each day, and staff members are culturally attuned to the need to avoid making direct opinions known or in any way contradicting a senior staff member. Senior staff and management are less likely to use indirect requests. Both verbal and nonverbal cues, made directly, are the norm. It would be very rare for a senior manager to ever be seen working alongside a para-planner during a given day. This firm's interpersonal culture can be defined as being based on *high power/distance* relationships.

The typical American financial planner would most likely find working for the Asian firm to be not only challenging, but, in fact, hostile. On the other hand, a Korean financial planner might find working in the American boutique firm to be puzzling and ambiguous. While both firms may be quite successful, these examples represent the extremes of a low power/distance and a high power/distance cultural perspective. The American firm reflects a cultural norm of equality and sharing among all staff members. The Asian firm illustrates a cultural preference for formality and high power structures.

Understanding cultural differences in relation to interpersonal preferences can have an immediate and long-lasting impact on a financial planner's success. Within many Asian cultures, for example, nearly everyone holds a high power/distance cultural perspective. Younger people are expected to be respectful of older individuals. Social status does matter as a form of power. This is the reason almost every financial services firm in Japan, China, and Korea, for example, uses a very formal, rigid, and complex meeting approach when working with clients. This tactic to providing financial planning services may work well when the general culture embraces conformity and control, but if the model were introduced into a culture that values low power/distance interpersonal relationships, the model might fail. The key takeaway is this: each financial planner's communication style must match that of his or her clientele. A financial planner, for example, who has a practice in a casual and even rustic locale, such as rural Nevada, would find it very difficult to succeed by establishing a firm based on a high power/distance model.

RISK MANAGEMENT

Culture and interpersonal communication also interact in the area of risk management preferences.[6] It is important to note that "risk" when used within communication theory does not refer to the level of loss someone is willing to absorb when faced with a decision that has uncertain outcomes. This is financial risk tolerance. Financial risk tolerance may be shaped, in part, by a person's cultural perspective, but this is a topic for another discussion. *Risk management,* as an interpersonal communication factor, refers to the manner in which someone deals with the ambiguity and uncertainty associated with social interactions.

There are cultural differences in the way people view *social risk,* which is broadly defined as the degree to which someone is willing to engage with others and share personal details with strangers. In general, people can be classified along a continuum as preferring to strongly avoid social risk or weakly avoid social risk, as shown in Figure 8.3. Many of the early client discovery discussions that take place during client–financial planner interactions provide a glimpse into a person's cultural risk preferences. Someone who prefers to strongly avoid social risk will tend to be more cautious when answering questions. They may also be less verbal and slower to respond to requests for information and background details. On the other hand, someone who was raised with a weak risk avoidance preference will be

FIGURE 8.3   Continuum of Risk Management Cultural Preferences

more willing to explore new ideas and answer questions freely. This type of person may also, with or without prompting, debate certain questions, answers, and assumptions.

Incongruent risk management perspectives between a client and financial planner can cause a financial planning engagement to end in frustration. A large number of financial planners working in the United States base their communication techniques on a weak risk avoidance foundation. That is, they expect their clients to be engaged in the financial planning process by answering questions directly and honestly. They anticipate that their clients will respond frankly and openly if a suggestion, recommendation, or implementation strategy seems inappropriate or risky. While this working assumption may be completely accurate in most cases, especially when the financial planner and client share a similar cultural background, trouble can quickly emerge when a client holds a strong risk avoidance cultural preference. Clients who, through cultural socialization, value strong risk avoidance can find the financial planning process confusing. Someone who is a risk avoider would prefer to have all assumptions, expectations, and other planning information presented in a direct and explicit manner. In other words, they would prefer (and expect) to know from the outset of the financial planning engagement what their role in the planning process should be and to then proceed within these very tight guidelines.

Consider how confused someone who wishes to avoid embarrassment or social misunderstanding would be if her financial planner said something like, "You are welcome to call the office at any time." Does this mean, for example, that the client is expected to call when she has financial questions? Does it mean that she should call on a regular basis, say, every two weeks? Or does it mean that there is really no need to be in touch until the financial planner reaches out to her? This level of ambiguity, associated with what many would view as a warm gesture of friendliness, could very well lead to the client terminating her relationship with the financial planner. As such, a financial planner who senses that his or her client is holding a strong risk avoidance cultural norm should take extra steps to ensure that information and expectations are explicitly communicated and understood.

Hwa-Froelich and Vigil[7] noted two things that should alarm financial planners. First, they reported that "cross-cultural communication inter-actions are at risk for causing misunderstanding and possible conflict" (p. 114). This is somewhat obvious. More alarming, however, was their observation that clients whose cultural norms do not match that of their financial planner, or when their adviser fails to recognize cultural differ-ences, may abruptly change financial planning firms. Stated another way, financial planners who will not or cannot account for the cultural unique-ness of their clientele may find that some clients will terminate the working relationship.

While these reflections are true of most professional associations, the reality is starker for those in the financial planning profession. Nearly all Americans, and those with a European ancestry, share a cultural perspective that is defined by independence, low power/distance prefer-ences, and weak risk avoidance. Increasingly though, prospective clients hold a cultural perspective that includes interdependence, high power/distance preferences, and strong risk avoidance tendencies. As illustrated in Figure 8.4, this can lead to direct conflict. Fortunately, conflict does not need to occur. Financial planners who use the communication tools and techniques presented in this chapter and throughout the book can take steps to better understand their clients' preferences and tastes. This includes learning not only about a client's financial situation, dreams, and goals, but also about their family background, cultural perspectives, and style preferences.

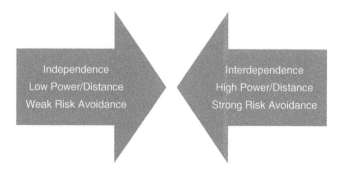

FIGURE 8.4 Possible Conflicts When Cultural Perspectives and Preferences Collide

CULTURE AND TRUST

An assumption underlying every tool, technique, strategy, and application presented in this book is that financial planners are interested in more than implementing a single transaction. The working proposition is that financial planners are concerned with creating long lasting, committed, engaged relationships with clients, or what is sometimes called a *working alliance*. At the core of this assumption is the notion of trust. Trust is one of those words that is extensively used but seldom defined. Here is a definition of trust that is both descriptive and insightful[8]: "*Trust* is a willingness to rely on another party and to take actions in circumstances where such action makes one vulnerable to the other party."

Trust is associated with concepts like honesty, benevolence, cooperation, and partnership, as well as uncertainty and expectations. To trust another person implies that there is some form of exchange involved in the relationship. The exchange may be monetary or social. As such, trust entails risk. The discussion that follows describes how trust can be developed. What is of critical importance, however, is the following insight from Hofstede[9]: whether trust in another person is established is based in large part on the social norms and cultural values that guide assessments, behavior, and beliefs. When a client and a financial planner share the same cultural values, preferences, and norms, the possibility for a trusting relationship to emerge increases dramatically. This is the reason a financial planner who some might consider too shy or timid to be successful may, in fact, be quite successful. That is, the financial planner has likely found a way to match his or her cultural norms and values to a particular client base.

It is important to remember, however, that cultural matching is not the only factor at play when developing a client–financial planner working alliance. It is possible for financial planners who hold, say, an independent cultural perspective to work well with clients who are more collectivist in nature. The key to trust development is changing the manner in which information is obtained and communicated between the financial planner and client. Equally important is being willing to adapt to the needs of a client. Being cognizant of client's cultural preferences, acknowledging differences, and altering the way in which planning is provided can be just as effective in creating a relationship based on trust as engaging with a client who shares basic core cultural values.

So, exactly how does trust develop? As shown in Figure 8.5, clients use one of five cognitive processes when engaging in trust building.[10] It is important to note that a client's cultural norms and values have a big role to play in determining which process is selected. As such, it behooves financial planners to be aware of each trust-building methodology and to be flexible enough to favor one over the others when it is an appropriate match with a client's cultural perspective.

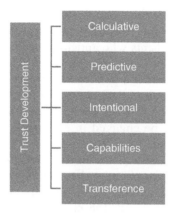

FIGURE 8.5   Five Cognitive Processes Associated with Trust Building

The first trust-building process is termed *calculative*. The approach gets its name from the process itself. Those who rely on the calculative approach perform a traditional *cost/benefit tradeoff analysis* when determining whether they should trust someone and to what extent their trust will be extended. Much of the logic behind the calculative method is based on *social exchange theory*. This theory suggests that individuals engage in estimates of relationship benefits weighed against costs. Benefits associated with the planning process include an increase in financial security, improved financial wellness, and hopefully, a rewarding association with a financial planner. Costs include fiscal outlays for planning services, time commitment, and potential interpersonal expenses (*vulnerability*) linked to sharing detailed and personal information with another person. Using this process of trust building, clientele should trust their adviser only to the extent that benefits outweigh costs. The calculative process should appeal to those people who believe that maximizing self-interests results in the most favorable outcomes for those engaged in a relationship. Clients who have a low power/distance and strong risk avoidance norm may not favor this trust-building approach.

Predictive models of trust are based on a client's ability to anticipate future actions of their financial planner. Because no one has a crystal ball for the future, those who rely on a predictive approach base their level of trust in a financial planner's past behavior and actions. Within this framework, trust should increase proportionately to a financial planner's *consistency of action*. Predictive processes that rely on the subjective estimation of probabilities appeals to those with a strong risk avoidance preference and those with a high power/distance norm. Also, clients who value interdependence are more apt to use a predictive process. Think of it this way: some clients need to know with a high degree of confidence how they will be treated and how their financial planner will act in any given situation. The more a financial planner rigidly meets expected outcomes, the higher the trust factor among clients who anticipate such outcomes.

Trust based on *intentional* processes is akin to assessing the sincerity of another person. Consider a financial planner who dresses in expensive suits, drives a pricey car, and flashes signs of wealth during a preliminary meeting with a new client. If the client's trust-building process involves intentionality, she will be engaged in evaluating the financial planner's motives and linking motives to factors such as benevolence, selfishness, altruism, and other characteristics. In this case, the financial planner will only gain the trust of the client if the client's assessment indicates that the financial planner is exhibiting these signs of wealth for the client's benefit. If, on the other hand, the client interprets the financial planner's actions as being self-serving or geared to flaunting his or her own wealth, trust will evaporate. Intentional processes appeal to those whose cultural norms include interdependence, low power/distance, and strong risk avoidance.

Intentionality, as a process of trust building, is most prone to misinterpretation from a cultural context. In the situation just described, some prospective clients will be impressed at the financial planner's apparent wealth. They may very well equate signs of wealth indicators of planning acumen. This could lead to assessing the financial planner's actions as a positive sign that they too will receive financial wealth by association. Clients whose cultural norm encompasses independence, high power/distance, and weak risk avoidance may, in fact, find this type of financial planner action appealing. On the other hand, prospective clients who are looking for a more egalitarian and low power/distance relationship may find the flaunting of financial planner wealth off-putting. These clients may perceive the wealth as ill-gotten or obtained unfairly at the expense of clients.

Trust built on *capabilities* is something that generally appeals to clients with a cultural norm of independence, high power/distance, and strong risk avoidance, although the method can also appeal to those who have a weak power/distance preference. Capabilities are what some might call *technical expertise*. Using this process of trust-building, a financial planner must signal to a client that he or she has the specialized skills and abilities to meet the client's obligations and expectations. Signals of expertise can include education, certifications, continuing education, and affiliations. For example, a financial planner who teaches at a prestigious university may be perceived as being more capable than another financial adviser. Other signs of capability include presentations of stability and long-lasting community relationship as evidenced by the office environment and institutional support of community groups and projects.

The fifth process of trust building involves *transference*. The concept of transference was introduced earlier in the book. In the context of trust building, transference refers to clients viewing a financial planner as trustworthy based on the financial planner's affiliation with another source. A prime example includes the Certified Financial Planner (CFP®) mark. Consumers are increasingly linking financial planning competence and ethical practice procedures with those who hold the CFP certification or another designation such as the ChFC, AIF®, or AFC®. In this manner, financial advisers who are also Certified Financial Planner practitioners receive a "positive glow" from the third party. In effect, the *certification* adds perceived credibility and helps create a sense of trust with some clients. Two points are worth considering. First, trust by transference is only effective in cultures that have high regard for the third party. There are, for example, hundreds of financial planning certifications and designations, but only a few carry the full weight and value of transference. Second, transference only works to add initial trust to the client–financial planner relationship. In some respects, transference is a short-term differentiator. It is essential that a financial planner build upon the established trust using one of the other trust-building processes. Transference appeals to a broad range of clientele but most specifically to those who value interdependence and group membership, low power/distance, and strong risk avoidance.

Even though it is tempting to think that a client will use only one process of trust building, in actuality, prospective and current clients use all five processes at some point when determining whether they will trust a financial planner and how much trust they will give in a relationship. Financial planners, likewise, undertake similar evaluations of their clientele. Table 8.1 illustrates how the methods of trust building interact with the six forms of cultural preference.

TABLE 8.1   Cultural Preferences and the Formation of Trust

	Trust Building Process Appeals to Those Who Prefer...					
	Independence	Interdependence	Low Power/ Distance	High Power/ Distance	Weak Risk Avoidance	Strong Risk Avoidance
Calculative	✓			✓	✓	
Predictive		✓		✓		✓
Intentional		✓	✓			✓
Capability	✓			✓		✓
Transference		✓	✓			✓

What is most striking about Table 8.1 is the extent to which the processes of trust building differ from cultural norms within the profession of financial planning. Think, for example, of a group of financial planners. If asked, most observers in this situation would tend to classify the financial planners as having a cultural preference for (1) independence, (2) low power/distance preferences, and (3) weak risk avoidance. Stated another way, financial planners, as a group, tend to be independent minded and informal team builders who have a willingness to take interpersonal risks. Financial planners, as such, are drawn to trust-building processes that are based on calculations, capabilities, and to some extent intentionality.

Contrast this to the way the majority of consumers develop trust. Consumers in the marketplace generally have a strong social risk avoidance preference. They also like to conform to standards, procedures, and perceptions. In other words, consumers, for the most part, are drawn to interdependent relationships. Consumers, especially those with low levels of financial knowledge and expertise, are also drawn to processes that are built on a high power/distance foundation. The typical prospective client, for better or worse, is looking for a high power expert.

What happens then when a typical financial planner meets a prospective client who is not of the same cultural background or holds divergent cultural norms and standards? If the financial planner is unprepared for or unacquainted with the interaction between trust building and cultural preference, an opportunity to connect with the prospective client could be lost. In all likelihood, the financial planner may attempt to build trust by presenting outcomes associated with the planning process as more beneficial than the costs associated with planning. They may also highlight their capabilities as a financial planner. The use of either a calculative or capability process will certainly appeal to some clients, but not always. If the client's cultural background is more attuned to interdependence or strong risk avoidance, the calculative method will fall on deaf ears. The prospective client may appreciate some forms of capability positioning, but this could be outweighed by other factors.

Had the financial planner taken the time to identify the cultural norms of the client, he or she may very well have altered what was presented to the client in terms of building credibility and cementing the client–financial planner relationship. Assuming again that the client is someone who values interdependence within the family structure, honors expertise, appreciates experience, and prefers to avoid embarrassing social encounters, then providing evidence that would support the client's use of predictive, intentional, and transference trust-building processes would be very appropriate. Again, as has been stated throughout this book, the use of nondirective and directive communication tools and techniques provide the basic framework to obtain information about a client, their preferred communication style, and cultural norms and values.

COMMUNICATION TABOOS

Cultural norms and values help establish what is appropriate behavior within a societal and occupational context.[11] Financial planners walk a fine line between being *culturally aware* and *culturally awkward*. This simply means that financial planners should not become overly preoccupied with creating an environment that meets the cultural expectations of every possible client who may walk through the door. It would be silly, for example, to jump from one discussion to the next using different questioning techniques, client-specific marketing materials, and unique staff interactions for every client. Not only would this be hugely time-consuming and potentially in violation of securities laws and regulations, the outcomes associated with the effort may not be worth the effort.

This does not mean, however, that financial planners should adopt an approach that requires clients to alter their cultural preferences in an effort to engage with the planner. A reasonable amount of give-and-take is not only appropriate, but is appreciated by clients. It really does not take much effort for a financial planner to learn a bit about a client's cultural preferences and then make adjustments to the way they work with those clients.

Financial planners can also be proactive when thinking about the types of clients they may work with in the future. Just as clients have a cultural preference for building trust, all societies have what are known as cultural kinesics. A *cultural kinesic* is any type of communication signal used in a discussion that relays specific information within the culture. Examples include *gestures, facial expressions,* and *posturing.* In an earlier chapter, these were described as forms of nonverbal communication. In this chapter, certain types of gestures, for example, are defined as culturally kinesic because of the precise language the nonverbal behavior communicates.

A CULTURAL EXAMPLE

A few years ago one of the authors was visiting South Korea with a group of American financial planners. The following is a brief account of how one behavior common in the United States led to an embarrassing situation overseas.

The purpose of the trip was to introduce financial planning practitioners from the United States to advisers in Korea. A key part of the trip involved having each of the U.S. participants give a presentation and sit on panels for the sharing of information. Unfortunately, one of the U.S. participants had a terrible allergy during the trip. While he was able to attend most meetings and answer questions, he was forced to blow his nose throughout each day. In the United States no one takes any notice if someone blows his or her nose. In fact, having someone clear his or her nose is much preferable to listening to that person constantly sniffling. However, in Korea (and many parts of Asia) blowing one's nose in public is considered rude. Actually, blowing one's nose in public goes beyond rude.

What makes this situation funny, in retrospect, is that the group had talked before the trip about gestures and behaviors that might be considered unpleasant or embarrassing. Blowing of the nose in public was one of those items. Yet, here was the group, day after day, with this person pulling out his handkerchief and tooting away. The clueless financial planner never made the connection between the giggles and the whispering that followed his incessant nose blowing. While no Korean said a word to him in private, the general perception was negative. Rather than being perceived as a financial planning expert, this gentleman was seen as "another oblivious American." Needless to say, he has not been invited back for further discussions or presentations by the Korean hosts.

Table 8.2 provides a summary of some of the most prevalent cultural kinesics that are known to send a particular message when used within a cultural population. It is important for financial planners to be aware of these messages because what one financial planner may consider to be an innocent gesture may be viewed as quite offensive or insulting to a client. This could lead to misunderstanding at best and the dissolution of the relationship at worst.

One aspect of Table 8.2 that is intriguing is that only a few of the nonverbal behaviors and gestures are universally taboo. Almost all behavior is culturally defined and geographically bound. As discussed earlier, financial planners need not be put off by the information in this table. Rather, the material is provided to help reduce possible embarrassment or misunderstandings.

TABLE 8.2 Selective Cultural Kinesics by Geographic Region

	South America	Asia	China	Europe	Russia	India	Japan	Mexico	Africa	Middle East
Hand Shake when Meeting Someone	✓	✓	✓	✓	✓	✓ Wait for Woman to Extend Hand	✓	✓ Wait for Woman to Extend Hand	✓ Wait for Woman to Extend Hand	✓ Wait for Woman to Extend Hand
Bow when Meeting	Unusual	✓	✓	Rarely	Rarely	✓	✓	✓	Rarely	Rarely
Embrace and Kiss on Cheek among Friends	✓	Rarely	No	✓	Rarely	Rarely	No	✓	✓	✓
Standing Close when Talking	✓	Rarely	Rarely	✓ No in England	✓	No	No	✓	No	✓
Pointing Index Finger at Someone	Rarely	Rarely	No	Rarely	Rarely	No	No	Rarely	No	Rarely
Winking	Unusual	Unusual	No	Unusual	Unusual	No	Rarely	Unusual	Rarely	No
Speaking Loudly	Rarely	Rarely	Rarely	Rarely France = Zero	Rarely	✓	Rarely	Rarely	No	No
	No	Rarely	Rarely		No	No	No	Rarely	No	
	✓									

(continued)

TABLE 8.2 (*Continued*)

	South America	Asia	China	Europe	Russia	India	Japan	Mexico	Africa	Middle East
Using Left Hand to Touch or Pass Something	No	Rarely	Rarely	Rarely	Rarely	No	Rarely	Rarely	No	No
Crossing Arms when Talking	Avoid	Avoid	Avoid	Avoid	Avoid	Avoid	Judged Hostile	Avoid	Avoid	No
Touching Person's Head	No	No	No	Avoid	Avoid	No	No	Avoid	No	No
Crossing Legs when Sitting	No	No	✓	✓	✓	No	✓	✓	No	No
Pointing Feet at Someone	No	No	✓	✓	✓	No	✓	✓	No	No
Pointing Sole of Foot at Someone	Avoid	No	Avoid	Avoid	No	No	Avoid	Avoid	No	No
Placing Arm on Back of Someone's Chair	✓	✓	No	✓	✓	✓	✓	✓	✓	Not if Person Is Female
Making Eye Contact	No	✓	No	✓	✓	✓	No	✓	No	✓
Remove Shoes Upon Entering a House	✓	✓	Rarely	Rarely	Rarely	✓	✓	Rarely	Rarely	✓
When Receiving Gift Use Both Hands	✓	✓ Thailand = Use Right Hand	Unusual	Unusual	Unusual	Unusual	✓	Unusual	✓	✓
Using Toothpick at Dining Table	No	Avoid	Avoid	Avoid	Avoid	Avoid	Avoid	Avoid	Avoid	Avoid

	South America	Asia	China	Europe	Russia	India	Japan	Mexico	Africa	Middle East
Blowing Nose at Dining Table	No	Avoid	Avoid	Avoid	Avoid	Avoid	Avoid	Avoid	Avoid	Avoid
Clearing Throat at Dining Table	No	Avoid	It is Okay to Burp after a Meal	Avoid	Avoid	Avoid	Avoid	Avoid	Avoid	
Arriving Late to Party	Acceptable	Unusual	No	Unusual	No	Unusual	✓	Acceptable; Visitors Should Arrive on Time	✓	No
When Offered a Drink, Say Yes	✓	Acceptable	Yes, Unless Female	✓	✓	Acceptable	Acceptable	✓	Acceptable	✓
Blowing Nose in Public	Avoid	No in Korea	✓	Avoid	Avoid	Avoid	No	Avoid	Avoid	Avoid
Standing with Hands on Hips	No	✓	✓	✓	✓	✓	✓	No	✓	✓
Unlucky Numbers		4 (Japan, Korea) 9 (Japan, Korea)	4 7	4 (Germany) 9 (France) 13 17 (Italy)	6					

Codes:
√ = Expected or acceptable
no = Not acceptable
Avoid = To be avoided
Rarely = Only occasionally a problem
Unusual = Seldom a problem

For those financial planning professionals working in North America, it is reasonable to expect clients to be adaptable to American and Canadian business customs. For example, it is acceptable and expected that an American doing business in a major U.S. city would shake the hand of a client when welcoming someone to their office. Unless it is obvious, for example, that a female client is uncomfortable shaking the financial planner's hand, it would be equally rude not to make a welcoming effort. As such, financial planners should not feel uncomfortable or restrained when working with someone of a different cultural background. It is perfectly okay to ask what is and is not culturally acceptable. In fact, asking about a person's history and background is one way to show concern and appreciation for a prospective client. Most people are excited to share information about their customs, history, and background.

SUMMARY

The concept of trust has been present in every chapter of this book. Nearly all financial planners strive to connect with clients at a deep, emotional, and impactful level of engagement. While it is true that a few financial advisers prefer to work with clients strictly on a transactionable basis, the financial planning process is designed to be managed at a deeper level. This requires open communication between client and financial planner. The end goal is the development of a trust-based client–financial planner relationship—a strong working alliance. As illustrated in this chapter, a person's cultural background, history, values, and norms influence both the communication process and the way in which trust is developed. As described here, cultural attributes can be split into three categorical preferences (responsibility, interpersonal, and risk management), with each consisting of additional elements (individualism/collectivism, low power/distance/high power/distance, strong risk avoidance/weak risk avoidance). These cultural perspectives are known to influence the manner in which people develop trust in financial planners. Five methods of trust formation were discussed (calculative, predictive, intentional, capability, and transference). The chapter concluded with a discussion of nonverbal cultural kinesics that sometimes create confusion, annoyance, or conflict between clients and planners. Although only a few of these gestures were noted to be in the realm of a taboo, all were shown to be of importance in helping financial planners develop relationships with clients.

CHAPTER APPLICATIONS

1. Cultural individualism represents what type of individual cultural preference?
   a. Responsibility
   b. Interpersonal
   c. Risk management
   d. Predictive

2. Swarn works in a medium-size financial planning firm. The firm is owned by a married couple who manage day-to-day operations. Swarn is responsible for the firm's marketing efforts, but on occasion he helps write financial plans. He likes the fact that the owners are willing to jump in and work on projects when needed. Based on this information, which of the following would best describe the firm's cultural perspective?
   a. Collectivist
   b. Low Power/Distance
   c. High Power/Distance
   d. Weak Risk Avoidance

3. Your best friend is considering hiring a financial planner to help work through some retirement planning questions. Your friend is not sure how much information to provide to the planner during the data-gathering phase of the planning process. She has created a list of the costs and benefits associated with hiring the planner. Without knowing anything else about the situation, you would say that her trust-building process is most likely:
   a. Intentional
   b. Predictive
   c. Calculative
   d. Independent

4. Your client has the following cultural preferences: interdependence, high power, and strong risk avoidance. Which trust-building process is he most likely to use?
   a. Capability
   b. Calculative
   c. Intentional
   d. Predictive

5. Later today you will be meeting with a prospective client. The client was born in Asia but is a recent U.S. citizen. You decide before the meeting to review your notes regarding cultural kinesic rules. Based on your knowledge of the situation, which of the following could be considered rude by the prospective client?
   a. Shaking the client's hand
   b. Blowing your nose during the meeting
   c. Offering the client something to drink
   d. All of the above

6. So-hyun is meeting her financial planner for the first time. She is very cautious, especially when it comes to talking about her financial situation. When asked a question by the financial planner, she takes her time in responding, is cautious in sharing information, and provides only the barest of details. Knowing this, which of the following is (are) true?
   a. She has a strong risk avoidance preference
   b. She has a weak risk avoidance preference
   c. She prefers a low power/distance relationship
   d. Both b and c are correct

7. Someone who is willing to rely on another party when making a decision that could make the decision maker vulnerable to the other party is known as:
   a. Trust
   b. Commitment
   c. Interdependence
   d. Independence

8. All of the following are costs associated with financial planning engagement from the point of view of a calculative client, except:
   a. Relationship with a financial planner
   b. Costs of services
   c. Time commitment
   d. Interpersonal vulnerability

9. Roger is searching for a new financial planner. He does not care about the race, ethnicity, or gender of his next adviser. He only cares that the person is highly skilled, particularly on issues related to small-business transition planning. Roger is most likely to build a relationship with a financial planner using which of the following trust processes?
   a. Intentionality
   b. Predictive
   c. Capabilities
   d. Calculative

10. Lily is flying to Europe to meet two potential high-net-worth clients. The first lives in France. The second lives in England. Lily tends to stand very close to others when she talks. In which country is Lily's communication style acceptable?
    a. France
    b. England
    c. Both France and England
    d. Neither France nor England

11. Use the categories in Table 8.2 to identify your personal cultural preferences. Think about a past situation in which someone asked you to trust him. Which trust-building process did you use at that time? Did your answer match the predicted process as shown in Table 8.1?

12. Notice that in Table 8.3 gestures and other forms of nonverbal communication are missing for Americans and Canadians. On a separate piece of paper, make notes regarding the acceptability of each cultural kinesic for North Americans.

Also add other communication items that those living in North America might find rude, intimidating, or uncomfortable.

13. Gather together with students in class or work colleagues. Arrange the seating in the room into a circle. Ask each participant to share with the group their name, nickname (if they have one), their ethnic or racial background, where they have lived, where they were born, where their parents were born, what U.S. generation they represent, and one or two cultural traditions their family practices. Before beginning, ask each participant to predict what the answers will be for at least one other member of the group. Keep track of the number of distinct and shared traditions, places of origin, or other information. Before concluding the meeting be sure to discuss what was surprising and helpful about what was shared.

NOTES

1. M. W. Kreuter and S. M. McClure, "The Role of Culture in Health Communication," *Annual Review of Public Health* 25, 439–455.
2. Id.
3. D. A. Hwa-Froelich and D. C. Vigil, "Three Aspects of Cultural Influence on Communication: A Literature Review," *Communication Disorders Quarterly* 25 (2004): 107–118.
4. G. Hofstede, *Culture's Consequences: International Differences in Work-Related Values* (Newbury Park, CA: Sage, 1984).
5. Id.
6. Id.
7. See Hwa-Froelich and Vigil, "Three Aspects of Cultural Influence on Communication."
8. P. M. Doney, J. P. Cannon, and M. R. Mullen, "Understanding the Influence of National Culture on the Development of Trust," *Academy of Management Review* 23 (1998): 601–620.
9. Hofstede, *Culture's Consequences*.
10. See Doney, Cannon, and Mullen, "Understanding the Influence of National Culture."
11. See id., 608.

CHAPTER 9

Politeness and Sensitivity in Communicating with a Broad Range of Clients

The financial planning profession has sometimes been accused of being exclusionary in the way planning services are delivered in practice. Whether this accusation is true or false, the reality is that many perceive that financial planning, as a profession, is less diverse than the general population and less sensitive to the needs of a broad spectrum of potential clients. One obvious strategy for the financial planning profession to overcome stereotypes and issues related to sensitivity and diversity is to facilitate the hiring of a more diverse workforce. The value of having diverse financial planning professionals—broadly defined and based on gender, age, racial or ethnic, religious, and sexual background—is inarguable high. However, ensuring that financial planning professionals, regardless of their background, can effectively engage people different from themselves may be of even more importance in helping additional households benefit from engaging in the financial planning process.

Although some clients will prefer to work with a financial planner who shares the same cultural background, it is likely that even more will not have this preference. Although published research on this topic, from a financial planning perspective, is lacking, research from other disciplines suggests this to be the case. For example, one study examining racial preferences for physicians found that about one-third of Hispanic Americans and about one-fifth of African Americans preferred their doctor to be of the same race or ethnicity. Said another way, over half of Hispanic Americans and the large majority of African American patients indicated that the race or ethnicity of their service provider did not matter.[1] Thus, not only is having racially diverse financial planning professionals extremely important, but also of great importance is having financial planners who have the communication skills to effectively serve clients of a different race, religion, or cultural background.

THE POWER OF LANGUAGE

The coding financial planners use in language can have a powerful impact on clients' emotions, and in turn, the client–financial planner working alliance. This is not just political correctness, although this is one component to sensitive communication. The coding of language is primarily referring to the power of nuance in the words a financial planner chooses to use when communicating with an increasingly diverse group of clients. The usage of polite and sensitive terms is overtly connected to the position that language represents. This includes thoughts and emotions. In other words, to create optimal communication with clients, financial planners should always consider contextual variables when encoding messages to ensure intent and impact are as congruent as possible.

VIDEO 9A

Video 9A shows an example of an insensitive comment made by a financial planner. In this example, the financial planner does not intend to be hurtful, but the language is interpreted by the client as disrespectful.

When a financial planning professional is impolite or insensitive to a client, the client may feel hurt, angry, or disrespected. It is important to mention that within the business world in general, *politeness* and *sensitivity* are widely recognized as important components of interpersonal communication, particularly within an increasingly diverse workforce. In fact, one recent study found that simply feeling respected was of primary importance to employees and associated with many positive outcomes such as reduced employee turnover, increased creativity, and higher work performance—all of which are quite beneficial to an employer's bottom line.[2] Thus, financial planners may want to not only focus on maintaining a high level of politeness and sensitivity with clients but also with other employees in their company or firm.

POLITENESS

Politeness, which encompasses behaviors and attitudes associated with consideration and respect for others, is viewed as a positive and desirable trait in the United States and across almost all other cultures.[3] As discussed in the previous chapter, however, cultures and clients may differ in how they perceive and appreciate politeness in contrast to, say, openness and honesty, or strength and power. With that said, some level of politeness is required to generate effective interpersonal communication and when building a strong client–financial planner working alliance, regardless of client and culture.

Joseph DeVito, a well-known author on interpersonal communication, suggests that it is helpful to consider politeness within the framework of both *positive politeness* and *negative politeness.*[4] Each form of politeness is responsive to one of two desires of clients. First, clients want to be viewed favorably and positively by their financial planner. This is referred to as *positive face.* Think about when you go to see another professional who has expertise in an area in which you do not, and you are paying for his or her services (for example, attorney, physician, business consultant). It is quite natural to want to be viewed favorably and respected by that professional. What makes you feel respected or liked? Do you (or does your firm) engage in these same behaviors in a systematic and consistent way? Second, clients usually desire to retain some level of autonomy and control. This is referred to as *negative face.* It is natural for clients to want to ultimately retain the right to do what they wish or to change their goals.

Having a financial planner as a professional partner has different meanings to different clients. Clarifying and possibly recalibrating expectations in regard to the decision-making components of the financial planning process may become necessary to ensure a client retains strong negative face. A financial planner who uses a high level of politeness when communicating with clients does so by allowing the client to maintain a high level of both positive and negative face.

More specifically, when a financial planner is practicing positive politeness by helping the client maintain positive face, the financial planner would speak very respectfully to and about the person. Simply saying "please," "thank you," not interrupting the client, and providing a client one's full attention are examples of providing positive politeness. In contrast, a financial planner could inadvertently attack a client's positive face by failing to fully acknowledge the client's opinions or expertise, forgetting to use the expressions "thank you" and "you are welcome," or sending messages that might challenge or undermine the image the client desires to portray. A financial planner explicitly stating to a client that he or she really respects that client for what he or she has achieved or the past decisions he or she has made is also effective in building a client's positive face. By maintaining a client's positive face, that client is more likely to be honest about his or her past and future goals, in contrast to embellishing what is true in an attempt to compensate to maintain positive face.

To help a client maintain negative face, a financial planner should regularly check in with the client about decisions regarding his or her financial plan. Instead of saying to a client, "I need you to come in at least once a quarter" a financial planner might say, "Would it be possible for you to come in to meet once a quarter?" Sometimes, a financial planner might inadvertently attack a client's negative face by challenging his or her autonomy. For example, a financial planner might say, "Are you really going to stop that automatic contribution to your IRA?" or "I need you to finish that paperwork this week." Although it may seem subtle, these statements weaken the negative face of the client and may jeopardize the client–financial planner working alliance. Rather, statements more conducive to supporting the client's negative face include:

> "Absolutely, we can make changes to your contributions as you wish. Would you like to meet to discuss how this might affect your overall financial plan or to discuss if there are other saving strategies to consider?"
> and
> "I wonder if there's anything we could do to help you with the paperwork; please don't hesitate to let us know if we can help or if you'd like to set up a meeting to complete the paperwork in the office."

Financial planners need to be particularly cognizant of supporting negative and positive face when engaging in directive communication. Maintaining both a client's negative and positive face through politeness in communication supports a strong working alliance.

The use of politeness, as a communication technique, is particularly useful when clients need to talk about really tough issues like religion, past financial mistakes, mental illness of a spouse or child, a job loss, divorce, or even marriage infidelity. The key here is to be face-saving and allow the client to maintain as much positive and negative face as possible. A financial planner can do this by focusing on not being evaluative of the other person. The financial planner instead should be empathic and effortful in trying to fully understand the client's position while at the same time not judging the client's emotions or personal views. For example, a financial planner may talk to a client about her religious beliefs, expressing clear interest without bringing any judgment or comment.

POLITENESS THROUGH INCLUSION VERSUS EXCLUSION[5]

At varying times, financial planners may consciously and unconsciously send messages of exclusion or inclusion to clients. *Exclusive messages* are generally considered impolite, as they directly or indirectly push someone out of the conversation, whereas *inclusive messages* are generally considered polite, as they are designed to acknowledge the presence of the client and keep them involved in the conversation.

It is not uncommon for financial planners to meet as a dyadic team—two financial planners in the room—with a client, which can provide a plethora of communication benefits but also greater complexity. For example, if one financial planner were to begin speaking to the other financial planner in the middle of a client meeting while using esoteric terms that a client might not understand, this would be an example of sending a message of exclusion. Obviously, there are situations in which it is appropriate and even beneficial for financial planners to speak to each other during a client session, but they should do so using inclusive messages. One way to do this is to break down any technical terms into common language the client can understand and thus follow, making it easier for the client to participate in the conversation. To further support a message of inclusion, the two planners should intermittently make eye contact with the client and periodically check in with the client to ensure they were following the line of conversation and are comfortable with the specific conversation as well as its pacing.

Clients can also receive and decode exclusion messages or impoliteness when financial planners overgeneralize terms specific to their own cultural or social groups. For example, the term *church* refers to place of worship for certain religions but it is not applicable to all religions. In other words, overgeneralizing the term church or bible to refer to all religious scriptures does not send a message of inclusion to a Jewish or Muslim client.

Consider the following dialogue between a prospective client who calls a financial planner to schedule a consultation meeting:

Client: "Hello, my name is Susan Smith and I'd like to make an appointment."

Planner: "Sure, Susan, I am happy to schedule a consultation meeting for you. May I ask if there are specific issues you would like to discuss?"

Client: "Well, I just got married so I was thinking it was finally time for us to put a financial plan in place with the help of a professional."

Planner: "Well, congratulations on the marriage, and yes, a financial plan is definitely something we can help you with."

Client: "Great!"

(continued)

(*Continued*)

Planner: "Before we schedule the meeting, could I please get your phone number and your husband's name?"

Client: [A long pause]…"Well, um, actually I just realized I don't have my calendar with me. Is it okay if I just give you a call back?"

Planner: "Sure, that would be fine. Have a great day and we look forward to hearing from you."

Client: "Okay, bye."

What potential messages of exclusion did the financial planner send during this conversation? Note how the financial planner assumed that Susan was in a heterosexual relationship by asking for her husband's name. Do you think that client is going to call back if she is married to a woman? This message of exclusion may deter the client from calling back, particularly when considering the natural tendency for people to overmagnify the meaning of information when only a small amount of information is available about the financial planner or firm (as discussed in Chapter 1). In the preceding dialog, simply asking Susan for her *partner's* or *spouse's* name could have achieved a message of inclusion and avoided the perception of being heterosexist through the use of insensitive language.

As this example illustrates, the use of words does matter. The terms *husband, wife,* and *marriage* refer to some heterosexual relationships, but exclude others. One of the authors recalls an assignment for financial planning students in a financial plan development course in which students were required to create a client questionnaire. Almost all the students included husband and wife labels within the questionnaire. Unfortunately, many online questionnaires from professional financial planners do the same thing. When this happens, the firm may be sending a message of exclusion to prospective gay and lesbian clients, as well as unmarried cohabiting heterosexual couples. Of course, using the terms *husband, wife, bible,* and *church* are all perfectly acceptable if a firm's intention is to communicate directly with a married, heterosexual, Christian couple, for example.

SENSITIVITY

Sensitivity in interpersonal communication is integral to developing and maintaining a strong client–financial planner working alliance. It is quite unlikely that a financial planning professional would self-identify as a heterosexist (as in the previous example illustrates), or an ageist, racist, or sexist, for that matter. It is likely, however, that he or she may be using certain phrases or communicating in ways that are consistent with these positions. This is due in large part to the fact that these issues unfortunately permeate our culture and thus unconsciously make their way into the coding of language. Part of the challenge is that financial planners and other professionals are often insensitive without realizing they are being insensitive. Remember, long-standing dominant cultural practice likely leaves a powerful, sometimes unconscious, influence over the most conscientious financial planner. Thus, even the most experienced financial planners have opportunities for improvement when the issue of sensitivity in client communication comes up.

For most professional financial planners, the concern will not be about obviously inappropriate characterizations or treatment of people based on gender, race, age, and other characteristics. Rather, it is the more subtle variations in language, body language, and communication among financial planning professionals that can be perceived as insensitive by a client that may be problematic. There are countless examples of the subtleties of expressions that, with no malicious intent, can have a remarkably adverse effect on a client. Consider the following dialog between a financial planner and this client:

Planner: "Do you have kids, and if so, could you share a little about them?"

Client: "We have two adult daughters, one who has two children, and one who has struggled with some medical issues, specifically with a disease called schizophrenia."

Planner: "Okay, that's helpful. For the daughter with the two kids, what do she and her husband do for a living?"

Client: "Well, actually, she's a single mom."

Planner: "Oh, so does she struggle financially and need financial support from you?"

Client: "No, she's doing okay financially, working as a nurse practitioner."

Planner: "That's great, but should I assume your schizophrenic daughter is not able to work and needs your help financially?"

Client: "Actually, she's an attorney and does quite well financially."

As you reviewed this conversation, you likely noticed the financial planner made a number of insensitive assumptions regarding marriage, financial stability of adult children, and even the overall stability of someone who suffers from a mental illness. More sensitive and inclusive responses from the financial planner would likely make a remarkable difference in building and maintaining rapport with this client.

This is not to say that making assumptions will always lead to a negative consequence, but it is to say that when client–financial planner conversation involves a potentially sensitive topic, it is even more important for the financial planning professional to not project his or her values or make assumptions. You may have noticed the wording used by the financial planner in this example was sometimes insensitive. For example, a professional should never define a person by their illness or disability. For example, the client's daughter is a person with schizophrenia, not a schizophrenic person (as this implies this person is defined by the disease). Other issues worth noting were the financial planner's use of the term *husband* rather than partner (before knowing if *husband* was appropriate), and kids rather than children (particularly once the client used the term *children*), and failing to ask and then use the children's actual names. By using the children's names, the financial planner sends an implicit and explicit message that she or he really cares to know the client and those who are most important to her. Lastly, the financial planner failed to immediately acknowledge important components to what the client was saying, thereby sending messages of exclusion.

Improving one's sensitivity in communication requires increased knowledge, empathy, and a lot of practice. For example, incorrectly referring to a client as Hispanic when she identifies only as Latino, inappropriately referring to a person in a wheelchair as handicapped, even making reference to an "African-American surgeon" or "gay athlete" is perceived by many as racist and heterosexist, in that it implies at some level that it is unusual or not normal for an African American to be a doctor or a gay person to be an athlete.

LANGUAGE SENSITIVITY

As with all the techniques and skills mentioned in this book, sensitivity can be learned, and as the old adage says, "practice makes permanent." Undoubtedly, financial planners who have a solid understanding of the interaction between language sensitivity within client communication will be in a much better position when it comes to creating, maintaining, and growing their financial planning practice. Having this greater awareness will increase the probability that correct messages are encoded and decoded when communicating with clients. To a large extent, implementing the communication skills outlined throughout this book will facilitate more sensitivity when communicating with clients. The following discussion provides an introductory-level collection of concepts that are designed to provide financial planners with even greater awareness of issues related to language sensitivity. This is hardly an exhaustive list, but the following three important concepts inform sensitivity in language: ageism, racism, and sexism.

Ageism generally refers to prejudice against certain age groups, typically older adults, but a reference to all teenagers being irresponsible or materialistic is also an example of ageism. In many cultures around the world, older adults are regularly sought out for advice about all aspects of life. Unfortunately, in the United States, ageism is made evident through negative stereotypes and disrespect shown to older adults. The author Joseph DeVito brings home the point in the following passage:

> Popular language is replete with examples of linguistic ageism; "little old lady," "old hag," "old-timer," "over the hill," "old coot," and "old fogy" are a few examples. As with sexism, qualifying a description of someone in terms of his or her age demonstrates ageism. For example, if you refer to a "quick-witted 75-year-old," or "an agile 65-year-old," or "a responsible teenager," you're implying that these qualities are unusual in people of these ages and thus need special mention. You're saying that "quick-wittedness" and "being 75" do not normally go together. The problem with this kind of stereotyping is that it's simply wrong. There are many 75-year-olds who are extremely quick-witted (and many 30-year-olds who aren't).[6]

Of course, a financial planner should make adjustments when talking with someone who has hearing, language, or cognitive difficulties. However, to avoid ageist communication, it is helpful to reflect on one's tendencies to make assumptions and to intellectualize the illogical stereotypes that ageism (and all isms for that matter) are based on. For example, keep in mind the following *factual examples* that run counter to common stereotypes in the United States:

> - Most older people are cognitively very sharp, thus talking down to an older adult could easily be perceived as condescending or patronizing.
> - Most older people can see and hear very well. They may actually hear much better than their financial planner with the help of a hearing aid.
>
> *(continued)*

(*Continued*)

- Most older people are still interested in romantic relationships. Failing to ask about relationships could be a lost opportunity to build client–financial planner rapport.

Minority is a term that has been in widespread use since the 1950s. The term *minority* refers to specific racial and ethnic groups, and more recently, to nonethnic groups. To many, the term has been generalized to any group enduring oppression by another group with greater power. Most experts who write on the subject tend to agree with Wirth's (1945) definition: "[groups of people] who because of physical or cultural characteristics, are singled out from the others in the society in which they live for differential and unequal treatment" (p. 347).[7] Some financial planners may mistake the term *minority* as a reference to a numeric faction. This, however, is incorrect. For example, women in the United States are actually a numeric majority but are considered a minority group based upon the definition above.

There are many definitions for *racism* or racist language, but a common theme to nearly all definitions is when a person puts another person in an inferior position or holds a negative belief about that person based on their race or ethnic group. One minority group in the United States includes African Americans. Polls and surveys suggest that a majority of Blacks have no preference between the use of the term Black or African American; an individual, however, may have a preference. Many Americans in recent decades have observed Black History Month and many universities have a major or minor in Black Studies. With that said, learning and adapting to client preferences is considered a best practice in this regard.

When talking about sensitive topics or labels, a common maladaptive technique employed by some financial planners is *avoidance* or *deflection*. A more polite and sensitive approach is simply to ask the client about preferences in a caring way. In the authors' campus-based pro bono financial planning clinic, we use a common phrase to remind students of this approach: "when in doubt, shout it out," which is a good reminder to not overspeculate about a client's emotions or preferences. Simply ask, instead, when unsure.

Here is another example. Are the terms *lady* or *girl*, when referring to an adult woman, considered sexist when communicating with clients? *Gender-biased language* is undoubtedly one form of sexism. As one example, the American Psychological Association's publication manual indicates that the use of the term *girl* is only appropriate when referring to someone high school age or younger. Assuming a husband will be less sensitive or have less desire to be the caregiver of his children than his wife is also form of sexism. Some common tips to avoiding sexist language within discussions with clients are as follows:

- Avoid using gender-specific pronouns (for example, his, he) or the term *man* generically (for example, humankind versus mankind, staff versus manpower). When writing, a financial planner can alternate pronouns or simply remove them.
- Avoid communicating disproportionately with one particular gender when meeting with opposite-sex couples.
- Avoid making disproportionate eye contact with a particular gender when meeting with clients (for example, male financial planner making substantially more eye contact with the husband when working with a married heterosexual couple).
- Avoid sex role stereotyping (for example, making the assumption within hypotheticals that doctors are male and nurses are female or that elementary school teachers are female and college professors are male).

It is not uncommon for financial planners to struggle with sensitive communication around the issue of physical and mental disabilities. The American Psychological Association, through their widely used publication manual, recommends the following:

Avoid language that objectifies a person by her or his condition (e.g., autistic, neurotic), that uses pictorial metaphors (e.g., wheelchair bound or confined to a wheelchair), that uses excessive and negative labels (e.g., AIDS victim, brain damaged), or that can be regarded as a slur (e.g., cripple, invalid). Use people-first language, and do not focus on the individual's disabling or chronic condition (e.g., person with paraplegia, youth with autism).

Table 9.1 provides a few examples of insensitive and sensitive wording with the goal being to reduce bias in communication with clients[8]:

After reviewing the sampling of sensitive words shown in Table 9.1, some simple rules become apparent, such as remembering to always refer to the person first, not the disability. It is important to remember that term preferences relating to racial and ethnic groups, religious groups, and other groups often change over time. Thus, it is important to integrate periodic communication sensitivity training into your personal (and the firm's)

TABLE 9.1   Examples of Insensitive and Sensitive Terms in Communication

Insensitive Language	Sensitive Language
Girl, lady	Woman, womyn
Schizophrenics; a bipolar; mentally ill; mental disorder, insane	Persons with schizophrenia; person with bipolar disorder; a person with an emotional disorder
A quadriplegic	A person with quadriplegia
Sex	Gender
Slow learner, retarded	Person with a specific learning disability/ intellectual disability
Epileptic	Person with epilepsy, person with seizure disorder
Handicap parking, disabled parking	Accessible parking, disability parking
Hearing impaired, hearing impairment	Deaf, person who is deaf, person with hearing loss, hard of hearing
The blind, the deaf	The blind community, the deaf community
Crippled	A person with a (physical) disability, a person who uses a cane
Fireman, policeman, salesman, stewardess, chairman	Firefighter, police officer, salesperson, flight attendant, chairperson
Oriental	Asian
Indian	Native American
Homosexual	Lesbians, gay men, bisexual women/men
Afro-American	Black or African American (depends on preference)

professional development plan. This is why the following principles are so important:

1. When in doubt, refer to the person first, and
2. When in doubt, check in with the client on his or her preferences when communicating about sensitive topics.

SUMMARY

Remember, as mentioned in the previous chapter, clients who perceive their financial planner as similar to who they are personally almost always evaluate their financial planner highly in regard to competence, and ultimately, trustworthiness. This assessment tends to strengthen the client–financial planner working alliance. This is, in large part, why impolite and insensitive language can destroy the trust between a client and a financial planner. Inappropriate language can certainly lead to substantial tears in the working alliance.

It is important to remember that everyone has biases based on unique cultural backgrounds, family socialization, and exposures (or lack thereof) to different people. Fortunately, financial planners, through practice, can become even more polite, inclusive, and sensitive within the context of client–financial planner communication. Staying current is important, as language is always evolving. Ongoing learning and applying appropriate language is not just about being politically correct, but rather about being able to communicate in the most polite, inclusive, respective, and effective way possible. As previously mentioned, financial planners who have a solid understanding of the interaction between language sensitivity within client communication will undoubtedly be in a much better position when it comes to creating, maintaining, and growing their financial planning practice.

CHAPTER APPLICATIONS

1. A financial planner's *positive politeness* increases a client's *positive face,* which refers to which of the following desires of clients?
   a. To maintain a certain level of autonomy and control over financial decisions
   b. To relinquish all responsibility and control over their finances
   c. To be viewed favorably and positively by their financial planner
   d. To be viewed as challenging to the financial planner

2. A financial planner's *negative politeness* increases a client's *negative face,* which refers to which of the following desires of clients?
   a. To maintain a certain level of autonomy and control over financial decisions
   b. To relinquish all responsibility and control over their finances
   c. To be viewed favorably and positively by their financial planner
   d. To be viewed as challenging to the financial planner

3. Asaaf, a prospective client, has an MBA in finance from Wharton. However, he has worked as an organic farmer for more than 14 years, which he started on his own. All of the following statements would likely reduce the positive face of the client and potentially hinder the client-planner working alliance, except:
   a. "Wow, an MBA from Wharton is impressive, but too bad you don't get to use it."
   b. "Fourteen years is long time. I bet you've forgotten most of what you've learned."
   c. "Help me understand why someone with an MBA from Wharton would need the help of a financial planner."
   d. "Wow, an MBA from Wharton is impressive, and equally and more impressive is your entrepreneurship and success as an organic farmer.... It would be wonderful to partner with someone like you, who has so much business and financial knowledge."

4. All of the following statement would likely reduce the negative face of the client and potentially hinder the client-planner working alliance, except:
   a. "We are only willing to meet with you once a year to review our management of your accounts."
   b. "This is too technical for you to understand and you'll just have to trust me."
   c. "Don't invest one penny in gold."
   d. "We would like to meet to make sure you are fully on board before making changes to your investment strategy."

5. You are working with a married couple—a wife and husband who recently retired. You find yourself talking to the husband about this gun collection for over 20 minutes without making eye contact with his wife or checking in with her. Although you were likely building strong rapport with the husband, you were sending what kind of messages to the wife that may hurt your working alliance with her?
   a. Inclusive messages
   b. Exclusive messages
   c. Rude messages
   d. Incongruent messages

6. When meeting with a client who is Muslim, you found yourself commenting to your financial planner partner about churches close to the office. What type of messages were you potentially sending to your client?
   a. Inclusive messages
   b. Exclusive messages
   c. Rude messages
   d. Incongruent messages

7. When meeting with a client, you simplify any technical terms into common language the client can understand and thus follow and participate in the conversation. You also intermittently make eye contact with client and periodically check in with her to make sure she was understanding you and was comfortable with the pace of the conversation. What type of messages are you sending to the client?
   a. Inclusive messages
   b. Exclusive messages
   c. Rude messages
   d. Incongruent messages

8. What would be the most polite and sensitive terminology to use on an online data-gathering questionnaire for couples?
   a. Him and her
   b. Husband and wife
   c. Primary client and secondary client
   d. Client A, client B

9. Which of the following statements are false regarding older clients?
   a. Most older people are cognitively very sharp
   b. Most older people can see and hear very well
   c. Most older people are less interested in talking about goals
   d. Most older people are still interested in romantic relationships

10. While reviewing Table 9.1, make a list of additional terms that you believe some people may or may not find offensive. Conduct an Internet review to determine what has been written about these terms' usage and appropriateness.

11. Interview your colleagues about words they prefer when someone describes them. For example, does a Caucasian colleague prefer the term Euro-American, White, Caucasian, or some other term? After collecting information from your colleagues, check to see if the literature and the personal experiences of your peers coincide?

12. Over the course of a week, make a list of how many times during each day people are explicitly polite to you. At the end of the week, think about whether you felt and performed better when the number of polite interactions was higher or lower. What does this tell you about the use of language in shaping perceptions?

NOTES

1. F. M. Chen, G. E. Fryer, R. L. Phillips, E. Wilson, and D. E. Pathman, "Patients' Beliefs about Racism, Preferences for Physician Race, and Satisfaction with Care," *The Annals of Family Medicine* 3, no. 2 (2005): 138–143.
2. D. Tsiantar, "The Cost of Incivility," *Time* (February 14, 2005), B5.
3. P. Brown and S. C. Levinson, *Politeness: Some Universals of Language Usage* (Cambridge, UK: Cambridge University Press).
4. J. Devito, *The Interpersonal Communication Book* (Boston: Pearson Education, 2009).
5. Id.
6. Id.
7. L. Wirth, "The Problem of Minority Groups," in *The Science of Man in the World Crisis*, ed. R. Linton (New York: Columbia University Press, 1945).
8. United States Agency for International Development, 2007. Downloaded from www.usaid.gov.

10

Financial Planning—A Sales Perspective

The purpose of this chapter is to briefly introduce the concepts of selling and being a salesperson in the context of financial planning. This chapter is not about developing a marketing plan, identifying target clients, or memorizing sales scripts "guaranteed to close 20 percent of your client appointments." Instead, this chapter is designed to help financial planners understand that nearly every aspect of their day-to-day activities involves selling. The sale could be a simple as persuading an office manager to purchase a special snack for the break room or as complicated as getting a high-net-worth client to buy a deferred variable annuity. While the stakes and outcomes associated with these types of sales presentations are certainly different, the key elements of client communication and counseling are embedded in both sales presentations.

Sometimes those new to the field of sales inaccurately use the terms *marketing* and *selling* interchangeably. For the purpose of this discussion, *marketing* refers to the manner in which a firm or organization creates a message to facilitate the exchange of products, services, and values with consumers or stakeholders. Selling is a component of marketing. *Selling,* in the context of marketing, is a problem-solving endeavor.[1] When people, especially those just beginning their professional career, think about the possibility of becoming a salesperson, they often become anxious, concerned, and in some cases, alarmed. Why? The reason is that the terms *sales* and *selling* have come to be associated with negative perceptions. Consider the list of personal attributes and characteristics displayed in Table 10.1. Look at the terms in each row. Mark which word (for example, "honest" or "deceptive") comes to mind first when you think about the word "salesperson."

When asked, most people believe that each of the terms in the right-hand column (that is, deceptive, impulsive, fast talker, pushy, loud, and likes cold calling) are attributes and characteristics of salespeople. This

TABLE 10.1 Personal Attributes and Characteristics

1	Honest	Deceptive
2	Patient	Impulsive
3	Good Listener	Fast Talker
4	Humble	Pushy
5	Thoughtful	Loud
6	Likes Strategizing	Likes Cold Calling
	TOTAL	TOTAL

helps explain why very few people set out on a career in sales. These terms are not at all flattering or personal characteristics that are valued in society. The problem is, of course, that in this case perception does not match reality.

While it is certainly true that some salespeople—even high-performing salespeople—may be impulsive or fast talkers, these are not essential attributes associated with achieving success in sales, particularly in the context of financial planning. In fact, each of the attributes and characteristics shown in the left-hand column (that is, honest, patient, good listener, humble, thoughtful, and like strategizing) are exhibited by successful salespeople.

This last point is becoming even more relevant as the millennial population begins to accumulate more assets and economic power. The typical consumer today values, and is beginning to demand, consultative selling. The *consultative selling process* is focused on helping match a product or service to each customer based on each customer's personal characteristics, needs, and desires. This is a contrast to the more traditional *transactional sales process*. Those who use a transactional approach tend to focus on increasing their volume of sales. To do this, they often simplify the number and type of products and services offered. A "one size fits most" approach marks the use of a transactional model.

While there certainly are times and places when a transactional approach is appropriate, consultative selling is something that is beginning to dominate the financial planning marketplace. Current and prospective clients want to know that the advice they are being given is honest, fair, thoughtful, and based on the client's needs rather than what is best for the salesperson or salesperson's firm. The role of communication and counseling rises to the forefront for those who wish to use a consultative selling approach. This means that the salesperson must focus on being a good listener, thoughtful, and an effective counselor.

The remainder of this chapter is focused on presenting some of the most important aspects associated with blending communication and counseling skills into the sales process.

SALES MODELS

There are literally hundreds, if not thousands, of sales models and approaches being used in the financial planning profession. Some of these models are based on the features shown in Table 10.1. This book is certainly not advocating one sales or business model over another, but there are a variety of differences with each that may impact client engagement. Twenty years ago, for example, it was not uncommon for financial service advisers to be hired by the hundreds, trained for two or three weeks in sales principles, and then handed a phone book as a means to "dial for dollars." Cold calling was the primary way financial planners prospected for new clients. With this technique, only those who could handle rejection, survived for more than a few months. The premise of what was known as "killing what you eat" was that the salesperson did not necessarily need to know about a client's needs or goals, but rather, about how a product could be positioned and sold.

While there are still a few companies in a variety of professions that use these old-school techniques, most firms operating in the financial planning field have adopted more client-focused consultative sales approaches. The most successful financial planners certainly prospect for new clients, but the days of "dialing for dollars" are nearly over. Instead, the emphasis has turned toward cultivating current clients for referrals. This means that rather than viewing a client as a single transaction point that is valuable in terms of one or two product sales, the relationship a financial planner has with his or her clients is increasingly viewed as the asset. In other words, developing and strengthening the client-planner alliance is something the most successful financial planners strive to accomplish. An important element making up the value of a typical client relationship is whom the client knows. It is these individuals who may later become clients.

THE CHALLENGER MODEL

Today, a very common model used to educate financial planners in sales techniques is called the *challenger sales model*.[2] The model is based on the belief that consumers have access to more timely and diverse information that has increased their transactional power. In response, some firms have changed the way they approach potential and current clients. Firms that have adopted the challenger model approach segment the sales process into three categories: (1) teaching, (2) tailoring, and (3) controlling. The most succinct description of the process was presented by Adam Rapp and his associates[3]:

> *Salespeople need to "challenge" their customers in an effort to spur a different way of thinking and create a new mindset for buying... [with the] goal of creating a constructive tension between buyers and sellers.*

Within this model, the best salespeople tend to share the following characteristics:

- Strong communication skills
- Knowledge of what drives customer demand
- Offering clients unique perspectives
- Providing economic benefits associated with product implementation
- Applying pressure effectively

The challenger model is a significant improvement over older approaches that relied primarily on aggressive product sales techniques. An advantage associated with the challenger model involves having the salesperson take the time to learn about each client's needs using advanced communication skills. Also, when this technique is used effectively, the salesperson is not perceived by clients as simply an agent of a firm, but rather as someone with a high level of expertise who can provide, and is willing to provide, valuable problem-solving skills.

A significant drawback associated with the challenger model is that communication skills are designed to elicit information from a client for purposes that some might view as manipulative. Whereas the academic literature clearly shows that client trust and commitment, or what has been termed throughout this book as a working alliance, are enhanced when a financial planner uses communication and counseling skills effectively, an underlying premise of the challenger model is that building relationships with clients is less important and potentially counterproductive. Those who advocate using the challenger model approach argue that financial planning activities are essentially transactional in nature. The process of transactions is provided in Figure 10.1. As illustrated, those who practice the challenger model believe that clients need a product or service, they search for a provider, and they implement recommendations. As such, the client neither demands nor expects their financial planner to provide a working alliance.

Client Needs Something

Client Searches for Expert to Fill Need

Expert Recommends Solution

Client Implements Recommendation

FIGURE 10.1 The Challenger Model Process

Instead, what a client needs is someone to challenge paradigms and push a client toward recommendation implementation.

THE CONSULTATIVE MODEL

In many ways, the challenger model, while an improvement over traditional sales approaches, has done little to improve the perception of sales or salespeople. In response, and as suggested earlier, many financial planning firms have adopted a *consultative sales model* approach. This sales technique places the salesperson in the role of problem solver rather than the intermediary between a firm and a client.[4] The primary difference between the consultative and challenger models is that the consultative approach is not designed to be objectively focused on the placement of a product or service. Instead, salespeople who apply a consultative approach tend to be intentional in creating a strong working alliance with their clientele. This, in turn, supports optimal matching of products and services to the characteristics, needs, and wants of the client.

A consultative salesperson provides professional advice. This description fits well with generally accepted professional financial planning standards. When viewed this way, the separate roles of (a) financial planner as advice giver and (b) salesperson as implementer disappear. Rather than working toward the ultimate culmination of a product or service sale, a consultative financial planner is focused on delivering information and recommendations that are aligned precisely with a client's needs. Soldow[5] summarized the attributes and characteristics of a consultative salesperson as follows:

- An uncompromising listener
- An analytical thinker who presents solutions after understanding a client's objectives
- Focuses on communication skills rather than scripts
- Encourages questions from clients
- Encourages open dialog with clients
- Encourages recommendation implementation only when a product or service meets a need
- Rarely (if ever) manipulative

MANIPULATION VERSUS PERSUASION

At this point, it is worth thinking about the difference between being manipulative and being persuasive. Someone who is *manipulative* tends to (1) be focused on his or her own well-being, (2) talk more than listen to sell the attributes of a product or service, (3) be product oriented, and (4) create tension, fear, and anxiety rather than trust. A manipulative sales approach is designed to sell a product or service with little regard for a client's true need for the product or service. Someone who is *persuasive,* on the other hand, tends to be perceived as an expert, likable, and act in the client's best interest at all times. Persuasion is an essential element associated with being an effective financial planner. It is, after all, essential that clients actually move toward recommendation implementation. A persuasive financial planner understands, however, that not all recommendations involve the sale of a product or service. Sometimes recommendation implementation entails behavioral change and attitudinal adjustment.

CONSULTATIVE SELLING AND COMPENSATION

Consultative sales models work well regardless of the way a financial planner is compensated. Table 10.2 shows the most common types of compensation methods used in the financial planning profession. It is important to note that this book is not designed to recommend one compensation method over another relative to communication or any other component of a financial planner's ability to serve clients. The next example is designed to show how the consultative approach can be applied in practice.

TABLE 10.2 Models of Financial Planning Compensation

Compensation Method	Illustration	Consultative Sales Application	Example
Fee-Only	Client pays a fee based on (a) assets under management, (b) hourly charge, (c) retainer, or (d) some combination of factors.	Delivery of product is secondary to ensuring client is working toward goal achievement.	Recommend accelerating debt payments rather than increasing contributions to a brokerage account.
Commission	Client pays a percentage of the amount of product purchased.	Focus shifts from selling the most expensive product or service to finding the most suitable product or service to meet a client's needs.	Recommend the purchase of a return-of-premium term insurance policy over a whole life policy.
Fee-Offset	Client is charged a fee for plan development; the fee, however, can be reduced if products that pay a commission are purchased by the client.	The plan becomes the primary deliverable with product and service implementation secondary.	Recommend that product implementation be postponed until after client debts have been paid down.
Fee-Based	Client pays a combination of fees and commissions.	Rather than focus on the sale of a product or service, the focus shifts to matching products and services to each client's unique needs.	Recommend the use of passive investments rather than actively managed higher-cost investments.

Each of the communication tools and techniques presented in this book was designed to enhance each reader's consultative sales skills. As noted at the outset of this chapter, the term *sales* should not be viewed as a negative word. Everyone engages in the selling of something every day. For some, the sale is getting one's children to eat their vegetables. For others, the sale involves having a client purchase a multimillion-dollar face value life insurance product. Regardless of the product or service, or the expected outcome, the sales communication techniques used to persuade someone else to take action tend to be similar. The following discussion reviews some the factors that lead to client behavioral change within the context of selling.

UNDERSTANDING CLIENT BEHAVIOR

Each financial planning client is unique. Some clients use very rational cost and benefit analyses before making a decision. These clients weigh the financial, emotional, and opportunity costs associated with a course of action and then choose to implement an alternative only if they estimate the gain as being greater than the costs. Other clients base their implementation decisions primarily on emotional prompts. They may seek pleasure, comfort, or recognition when making a decision. For example, it is common for clients to seek out products and services of well-known financial planning firms. Working with brand name companies provides these clients with a sense of status, as well as comfort knowing that their choice matches that of other consumers. Other clients prefer working with boutique firms that signal exclusivity. Still other clients make decisions using mental shortcut *(heuristic)* approaches. They might, for example, determine a need and then seek out a referral from a friend or colleague.

When viewed holistically, there are four factors that influence the decision of clients to implement recommendations, or in the words of a salesperson, to buy:

1. The environment
2. The client's financial planning needs
3. The client's peers and network
4. The client's capacity

Environment refers to everything outside of the client's household, including the macro economy, political issues, regulations, and economic expectations. Client financial planning needs include those that the client has self-identified, as well as needs that may become apparent through the financial planning process. Peers and networks encompass social norms and expectations among those the client socializes with on a regular basis. Capacity refers to a client's financial ability to actually carry through on a planner's recommendations.

FIGURE 10.2 Client Needs that Shape Buying Behavior

According to Hutt and Speh,[6] these four elements are embedded in seven client needs. These needs are shown in Figure 10.2. Clients may be motivated to purchase products or services that reduce real or perceived risks. Examples include insurance, warranties, and personal training. Financial security, within the context of financial planning, is somewhat obvious. Clients have a need to ensure that they are on track to reach their current and future financial goals. Comfort refers to obtaining products and services that provide peace of mind or improve the household comfort and condition. Acceptance relates to a client's need to make decisions that match the social norms of peers and colleagues. Recognition is also important. Nearly all clients have a need to be recognized for making prudent and efficient decisions. Influence is related to having some sway in the ways peers and colleagues view a situation and in taking control of one's intentions. Finally, professional growth can be a motivating factor by prompting people to implement recommendations as a means to learn more and gain more control over their personal and professional situation.

It is not necessary that a single financial planning recommendation meet each of the client's needs, as shown in Figure 10.2. A financial planner ought to take steps, however, within the planning process, to incorporate product and service recommendations that satisfy several of these needs during the client–financial planner engagement. This is, of course, facilitated by the appropriate use of communication techniques as a way to determine when meeting a particular need is important. For example, a client may implement a retirement recommendation simply as a way to ensure that she or he is on track to meet her or his retirement income need. The same client, however, might be hesitant to commit to making a large charitable donation unless he or she is recognized publicly for the donation.

DEALING WITH "NO"

An important element when dealing with client behavior, especially as it relates to product or service implementation, is dealing with situations in which a client says, "No." Even when a recommendation is ideally suited for a client's situation, the appropriate communication techniques have been used, and multiple needs have been addressed, the client may refuse to take action. Whether stated verbally or nonverbally through inaction, the client is communicating one thing: "no."

Rather than view "no" as a criticism or a failing, it is worth remembering that sometimes a client is not ready to move forward in the financial planning process. He or she may be faced with a hidden barrier to implementation. Most often, these barriers emerge as a refusal to buy a product or service. Barriers to implementation can also appear as procrastination, aloofness, or even uncaring.

Buskirk and Buskirk[7] noted that a recommendation may conflict with one of the following three client issues.

1. The first is that a recommendation may be incompatible with the client's self-concept. For example, recommending that someone sell his or her Rolex watches to pay down credit card debt may be rejected by a client who is focused on signaling affluence to friends and colleagues. Such a sale could be construed as failure and diminution of status.
2. Second, a recommendation may generate discomfort by forcing a client to move away from his or her current lifestyle. A client, for example, may prefer to maintain his or her current insurance coverage even though the cost is high because of his or her preference for the status quo. Implementing an insurance recommendation may position the client to rethink many of his or her long-held assumptions and expenditures.
3. Third, a recommendation may cause a client to experience guilt. This can occur when a recommendation is made in an effort to fix a past problem that was caused by a client's inaction or poor behavior. Some clients may prefer to avoid taking action as a way to shield their self-image from acknowledging past mistakes.

As these examples illustrate, a client may know that he or she should take action but be unwilling or unable to implement a recommendation at that moment. According to leading sales and business consultants,[8] it still may be possible to help a client move beyond his or her current preference of "no" to eventually say, "Yes." The following strategies can be used to facilitate this process:

- Clarify why the client is saying "no" by asking if no means no today or no at any time in the future.
- Identify the recommendation feature that is causing the reaction by asking what element of the plan is causing the client to say "no."
- Ask the client to discuss the issue in more detail.
- Refocus the client by having the client describe his or her long-term goals and how implementing the recommendation helps lead to goal accomplishment.
- Ask permission to follow up with the client later about implementing the recommendation.
- Offer to defend the recommendation against criticisms the client might have.

Of course, it is also acceptable in some circumstance to accept the client's position by indicating that you understand and respect the decision. At that point, it is well worth the effort to present an alternative for the client.

THE ETHICS OF SELLING

Before closing this chapter, it is worth mentioning again that financial planners play an important role in their clients' lives. In some cases, a client's financial planner is his or her most trusted adviser. The weight of this responsibility is a heavy one. At a minimum, financial planners should follow and advance the field's practice standards. This means doing no harm to a client and keeping the client's needs and desire first and foremost in mind when crafting and communicating recommendations. The communication and counseling tools and techniques that have been presented throughout this book should never be used to manipulate a client into taking action that is not in the client's best interest.

Financial planners have an ethical (and sometimes legal) responsibility to do what is best for their clients. By extension, this means that while it is acceptable to prompt clients to change their behavior to achieve positive outcomes, it is never acceptable to force a client to purchase a product or service that does not clearly help the client progress toward his or her goal achievement. While the line between manipulation and persuasion is not particularly clear, one way to know when the boundary has been crossed, in terms of being a salesperson, is when a recommendation is made primarily to benefit the salesperson through compensation, awards, or recognition. It is never appropriate to alter information about a product or service to influence a client's decision. Likewise, a professional salesperson should never bad-mouth a competitor or colleague in an attempt to unduly influence a client. The old adage that a financial planner should recommend only strategies that they would personally implement for him- or herself is one way to ensure that the sales process corresponds with high ethical standards of practice.

SUMMARY

The word *sales* is sometimes construed among the general public as being immoral, nasty, and obnoxious. Perceptions of these sorts stem from a history of salespeople being trained to manipulate consumers into making purchases that are not always needed or valuable. The reality is, however, that every financial planner—regardless if the person is a behind-the-scenes para-planner or a firm's CEO—is engaged in the process of selling. The para-planner, for example, needed to sell him- or herself in order to be hired. The CEO must sell herself daily to clients, regulators, and those in the media. Even those who do not work directly with the public are engaged in daily sales activities. The manner in which vendors are selected and retained and the level of service rendered and acquired are all based on relationships that start with one or more people selling their vision of the future to other people.

A key takeaway from this chapter is that being involved in financial planning sales is a good thing. Selling financial planning products and services provides an overall social good by enhancing the financial well-being of individuals and families. A financial planner is a problem solver. The best financial planners are those who are able to exhibit great listening skills. They are also analytical thinkers and outstanding communicators. The end result for those who are able to do these things well is a hoped-for outcome of nearly all practicing financial planners—creating a clientele that is engaged, committed, and willing to take action. Adopting a consultative sales approach that includes all of the tools and techniques described in this book is an important step in helping build strong client-planner engagements and equally strong working alliances.

CHAPTER APPLICATIONS

1. When a financial planner creates a plan that includes a profile of prospective clients and the type of messages that will be delivered, the financial planner is engaged in:
   a. Sales
   b. Marketing
   c. Manipulation
   d. Persuasion

2. Which of the following statements is (are) true?
   a. An important attribute associated with being a successful salesperson is being impulsive.
   b. Successful salespeople are rarely humble.
   c. Effective salespeople are problem solvers, which is one reason they often like to strategize.
   d. Both a and b are correct.

3. The most effective way to prospect for new clients involves:
   a. Cold calling
   b. Applying pressure on clients to refer new business
   c. Persuading new clients to transfer assets through seminars
   d. Building strong client-planner alliances

4. Within the challenger sales model a financial planner should focus on which of the following factors?
   a. Teaching clients about products and services
   b. Creating tension between the client and financial planner
   c. Building a strong working alliance
   d. Both a and b

5. Those who advocate the use of the challenger sales model believe:
   a. That it is appropriate to pressure a client into purchasing a product or service.
   b. That a salesperson should spend the maximum amount of time possible building a strong client-planner relationship.
   c. That clients should be allowed to engage in open dialog with the salesperson through ongoing questioning of recommendations.
   d. All of the above are true.

6. A financial planner who uses the consultative sales model when working with clients sees his or her work primarily as a(n):
   a. Problem solver
   b. Persuader
   c. Manipulator
   d. Implementer

7. A financial planner who charges a fee for writing a financial plan but then reduces the fee if the client purchase products or services from the planner is operating under what type of compensation structure?
   a. Fee-only
   b. Fee-offset
   c. Fee-based
   d. Commission

8. Assume a client is willing to implement a recommendation, but when the day comes to take action the client does not follow through with that intention. When asked why no action is being taken, the client responds that she and her husband lost a significant amount in their business. Lack of implementation due to this reason is called:
   a. Peer and network influence
   b. Client capacity
   c. The environment
   d. Client feelings

9. Toni has been retired for several years. She continues, however, to maintain membership in her former professional association. The membership fees are quite high, and this is straining her budget. When asked why she continues to retain membership, she says, "Because I can still influence the way decisions are made within the organization." Toni's answer reflects what type of behavioral need?
   a. Professional growth
   b. Comfort
   c. Acceptance
   d. Influence

10. Why might a client say "no" to a recommendation?
   a. The recommendation conflicts with the client's self-concept.
   b. The recommendation refocused the client on the achievement of long-term goals.
   c. The recommendation may prompt the client to feel guilty.
   d. Both a and c are correct.

11. Which of the following statements would be considered manipulative or persuasive?
   a. "I think Jane is an excellent financial planner. I've heard rumors, though, that she may be in trouble with the Securities and Exchange Commission."
   b. "I have been selling mutual funds for over 10 years. I can say, without a doubt, that this fund is the best mutual fund in the marketplace."
   c. "Implementing this recommendation will maximize your cash flow position, but if you don't feel now is the right time, the alternative recommendation can still be implemented in such a way that your cash flow situation will be improved."
   d. "Don't tell my manager, but I think I can swing a deal for you if you transfer funds into the account today."

NOTES

1. V. L. Singh, A. K. Manrai, and L. A. Manrai, "Sales Training: A State of the Art and Contemporary Review," *Journal of Economics, Finance and Administrative Science* 20 (2015): 54–71.
2. A. Rapp, D. G. Bachrach, N. Panagopoulos, and J. Ogilvie, "Salespeople as Knowledge Brokers: A Review and Critique of the Challenger Sales Model." *Journal of Personal Selling & Sales Management* 34 (2014): 245–259.
3. Id.
4. G. F. Soldow, *Professional Selling: An Interpersonal Perspective* (New York: Macmillan, 1991).
5. Id.
6. M. D. Hutt and T. W. Speh, *Business Marketing Research: B2B* (Chicago: Dryden, 2009).
7. R. H. Buskirk and B. D. Buskirk, *Selling: Principles and Practices* (New York: McGraw-Hill, 1992).
8. www.bizmove.com/manager-skills-tips/selling-to-prospective-customer.htm.

Solutions

CHAPTER 1

Multiple-choice solutions:

1. c	5. b	9. a
2. a	6. b	10. c
3. d	7. d	
4. c	8. a	

CHAPTER 2

Multiple-choice solutions:

1. c	5. d	9. c
2. b	6. a	10. a
3. d	7. b	
4. b	8. d	

Matching solutions:

6a. affective	6d. stable	6f. exploratory or
6b. orientation	6e. orientation	affective
6c. exploratory		

Matching solutions:

7a. appreciative	7d. problem
7b. problem	7e. problem
7c. appreciative	

CHAPTER 3

Multiple-choice solutions:

1. b	5. c	9. d
2. d	6. d	10. b
3. d	7. a	
4. d	8. d	

CHAPTER 4

Multiple-choice solutions:

1. d	5. a	9. b
2. c	6. c	10. d
3. d	7. a	
4. d	8. c	

CHAPTER 5

Multiple-choice solutions:

1. b	5. b	9. a
2. c	6. d	10. d
3. a	7. c	
4. d	8. c	

Solutions:

1. a	4. b	7. a
2. d	5. b	8. e
3. a	6. c	

CHAPTER 6

Multiple-choice solutions:

1. b	5. d	9. a
2. a	6. a	10. d
3. c	7. b	
4. c	8. c	

Matching solutions:

a1	g2	m3
b3	h2	n1
c2	i1	o1
d2	j3	p3
e3	k3	
f2	l3	

CHAPTER 7

Multiple-choice solutions:

1. b	5. c	9. c
2. b	6. a	10. a
3. a	7. c	
4. c	8. d	

CHAPTER 8

Multiple-choice solutions:

1. a	5. b	9. c
2. b	6. a	10. a
3. c	7. a	
4. d	8. a	

CHAPTER 9

Multiple-choice solutions:

1. c	4. d	7. a
2. a	5. b	8. d
3. d	6. b	9. c

CHAPTER 10

Multiple-choice solutions:

1. b	5. a	9. d
2. c	6. a	10. c
3. d	7. b	
4. d	8. b	

Statements a, b, and d are manipulative; statement c is persuasive.

About the Authors

John E. Grable, PhD, CFP
Professor and Athletic Association Endowed Professor of Financial Planning
Department of Financial Planning, Housing, and Consumer Economics
University of Georgia

Professor John Grable teaches and conducts research in the Certified Financial Planner Board of Standards Inc. undergraduate and graduate programs at the University of Georgia, where he holds an Athletic Association Endowed Professorship. Before entering the academic profession, he worked as a pension and benefits administrator and later as a financial planner in an asset management firm. Dr. Grable served as the founding editor for the *Journal of Personal Finance* and co-founding editor of the *Journal of Financial Therapy*. He is best known for his work on financial risk-tolerance assessment, behavioral financial planning, and evidence-based financial planning clinical studies. He has been the recipient of several research and publication awards and grants, and is active in promoting the link between research and financial planning practice, where he has published more than 100 refereed papers, co-authored three financial planning textbooks, co-authored a communication book, and co-edited a financial planning and counseling scales book. He also serves as the director of the Financial Planning Performance Lab at the University of Georgia. More information on his research and lab can be found at www.fpplab.org.

Joseph W. Goetz, PhD
Associate Professor
Department of Financial Planning, Housing, and Consumer Economics
University of Georgia

Dr. Joseph Goetz is an associate professor of financial planning at the University of Georgia (UGA), where he currently teaches undergraduate and graduate courses in financial counseling and client communication, and practice management. He is also a founding principal at Elwood & Goetz Wealth Advisory Group, an independent, comprehensive financial planning firm. He has co-authored more than 50 peer-reviewed publications in the financial planning and counseling field, and received the Richard B. Russell Excellence in Teaching Award. Dr. Goetz served as the 2013 president of the

Financial Therapy Association, and was recognized as the 2013 Financial Counselor of Year by the Association of Financial Counseling and Planning Education. He is also the co-founder of the university-based ASPIRE clinic, which provides pro bono financial planning services and a unique experience for students to develop their client-financial planner communication skills. He currently serves on the editorial boards of the *Journal of Financial Counseling and Planning,* the *Journal of Financial Planning,* the *Journal of Financial Therapy,* and the *Journal of Personal Finance.* He studied at the University of Missouri–Columbia, the University of North Carolina–Chapel Hill, and Texas Tech University. He has also completed three graduate degrees in the fields of psychology, financial planning, and economics.

ABOUT THE EDITOR

Dr. Charles Chaffin is Director of Academic Programs and Initiatives for CFP Board and Director of Academic Home, CFP Board Center for Financial Planning. He provides guidance and oversight to the 375 CFP Board Registered Programs as well as leads the academic initiatives such as the *Academic Research Colloquium for Financial Planning and Related Disciplines,* the upcoming new CFP Board academic journal, CFP Board book series, and other academic initiatives within the CFP Board Center for Financial Planning. His research has focused on the cognitive workload of learners in different task settings, reflective practice, and best practices in higher education curriculum and instruction, both within education as well as within financial planning. He is also editor of the first and second editions of the *Financial Planning Competency Handbook,* published by Wiley. He holds a master's degree from the University of Michigan and a Doctor of Education degree from the University of Illinois at Urbana-Champaign.

About the Companion Website

This book includes a companion website, which can be found at www.wiley.com/go/communessentials. Enter the password: grable234. This website includes the following videos:

1. 3A & 4A_Taking Notes, Listening Carefully, and Positive Body Language .mp4
2. 4B.1_Negative Body Language.mp4
3. 4B.2_Negative Body Language.mp4
4. 4B.3_Negative Body Langugae.mp4
5. 4C.1_Transference_correctly addressing.mp4
6. 4C.2_Transference_incorrectly addressing.mp4
7. 4D.1_Silence_correct use.mp4
8. 4D.2_Silence_incorrect use.mp4
9. 5A_Open-Ended Questions.mp4
10. 5B_Closed-Ended Questions.mp4
11. 5C.1_Swing Questions.mp4
12. 5C.2_Swing Questions.mp4
13. 5D_Implied Questions.mp4
14. 5E_Projective Questions.mp4
15. 5F_Scaling Questions.mp4
16. 6A_Reflection Statement.mp4
17. 6B_Summary Statement.mp4
18. 6C_Simple Paraphrase.mp4
19. 6D_Paraphrasing.mp4
20. 7A_Reframing.mp4
21. 7B_Reframing & Explanation.mp4
22. 7C.1_Advice - Correct.mp4
23. 7C.2_Advice - Incorrect.mp4
24. 7D_Urging Action.mp4
25. 9A.1_Insensitive Comments.mp4
26. 9A.2_Insensitive Comments.mp4
27. 9A.3_Insensitive Comments.mp4

Index

Page numbers followed by *f* and *t* refer to figures and tables, respectively.

Lightning Source UK Ltd.
Milton Keynes UK
UKHW011259230819
348368UK00001B/2/P